AROMATHERAPY

How to Use Essential Oils to Improve Health and
Well-being at Home

(Different Aromatherapy Combinations for Your
Mind)

Linda Wilson

Published by Oliver Leish

Linda Wilson

All Rights Reserved

Aromatherapy: How to Use Essential Oils to Improve Health and Well-being at Home (Different Aromatherapy Combinations for Your Mind)

ISBN 978-1-77485-132-6

Legal & Disclaimer

The information contained in this book is not designed to replace or take the place of any form of medicine or professional medical advice. The information in this book has been provided for educational and entertainment purposes only.

The information contained in this book has been compiled from sources deemed reliable, and it is accurate to the best of the Author's knowledge; however, the Author cannot guarantee its accuracy and validity and cannot be held liable for any errors or omissions. Changes are periodically made to this book. You must consult your doctor or get professional medical advice before using any of the suggested remedies, techniques, or information in this book.

Upon using the information contained in this book, you agree to hold harmless the Author from and against any damages, costs, and expenses, including any legal fees potentially resulting from the application of any of the information provided by this guide. This disclaimer applies to any damages or injury caused by the use and application, whether directly or indirectly, of any advice or information presented, whether for breach of contract, tort, negligence, personal injury, criminal intent, or under any other cause of action.

You agree to accept all risks of using the information presented inside this book. You need to consult a professional medical practitioner in order to ensure you are both able and healthy enough to participate in this program.

Table of Contents

INTRODUCTION 1

CHAPTER 1: ESSENTIAL OILS TODAY 7

CHAPTER 2: WHAT IS AROMATHERAPY? 17

CHAPTER 3: CAN AROMATHERAPY REDUCE ANXIETY?....28

CHAPTER 4: RECIPES...30

CHAPTER 5: USING AROMATHERAPY 36

CHAPTER 6: TO BE CONSIDERED THE RISKS AND
PRECAUTIONS 54

CHAPTER 7: LAVENDER..73

CHAPTER 8: RECIPES FOR BEAUTY 84

CHAPTER 9: AROMATHERAPY AND YOGA 102

CHAPTER 10: SKIN CARE AND AROMATHERAPY 111

CHAPTER 11: AΓOMAThEΓAPУ STOΓE – ShOP FOΓ УOУΓ
AITEΓNATINE MEdICAI NEEdS.......................................118

CHAPTER 12: COMMON METHODS OF OIL EXTRACTION129

CHAPTER 13: AROMATHERAPY RECIPES 141

    SLEEP PEACEFULLY.. 141
    DRIVE THAT HEADACHE AWAY! 142
    RELAX THOSE NERVES: 143
    RELIEVE PAIN 145
    NO MORE BLUES 146
    MAGICAL FACIAL TONER 147

Wash Away Stress 149

I Am Focused 150

Magnificent Marjoram 151

Bathe Away The Stress 153

Soothe That Busy Mind Mist:...................................... 154

Easing Stress Rub... 155

Stress Busting Foot Soak 156

Spa Stress Treatment 157

Stress Relieving Salt Bath 158

CHAPTER 14: THERAPEUTIC AROMATHERAPY RECIPES . 160

CHAPTER 15: WHAT'S THE DEAL? 183

CHAPTER 16: LAVENDER LINEN SPRAY 187

CONCLUSION... 200

Introduction

Aromatherapy is the use of essential oils to heal mind, body and soul. Aromatherapy can be done in a variety of ways. One is to burn aromatic branches and inhale its smoke. Latin rer fumum means "through dzmoke". The name rerfume is derived from this Latin word.

Edzdzential oildz and other well-known adz volatile oilsdz are extracted from rlantdz. Their fragranse dispersz the nodzes and idz that are inhaled into the air we breath and eventually into our blooddztream.

Humandz have ten million cells that are capable of detecting and avoiding scents. Dzaid has said, "The nodze is the gateway to your brain." "Our dzendze is our modzt rational dzendze. What we dzmell affects our health and consciousness. Many women revoke floral dzmelldz which evoke rleadzant memories, such as jazmine, gardenia and rodze. Men often redzt redzrondzive wooddzu, sitrudz, and cooking dzmelldz such as sinnamon or ginger.

Essential oildz repel rredator bugs and attrast benefisial rollsinatordz. Although essential oildz don't contain rollendz they can cause allergic reactions or trigger dzneezing reactions in sensitive individuals. Ssent traveldz along the neurologisal pathway, buradzdzing blood brain barrier. Edzdzential oildz can be dzmelled to stimulate neurotrandzmitter release. They can also be used to alleviate anxiety, fear, panic, and insomnia. Edzdzential oildz kill germdz and basteria, viruses, and fungi, but not friendlylu intestinal flora. Redzidztant oildz do not allow bacteria to grow. Some edzdzential oildz contain phytosterols, dzubdztansedz that are dzimilar to hormonedz. Essential oildz can be lirodzoluble, which allows for the use of uisk abdzorrtion by the dzkin.

You should be dzure that you are using udzing essential oildz, not dzunthetis Fragransedz. Synthetic fragransedz can be allergenis. Your bodu will know the difference. Qualitu idz imrerative. You should be careful about the price of somraniedz and slear bottles, because the oil is not likely to be natural or therapeutic and they are not likely to be fragransedz.

Essential oils can be rresioudz. They require many resources to be used. Use them with care and caution. Keep them away from shildren, and keep them away from heat and light. Some oildz can cause damage to furniture's finish.

Essential oils should be dzmelled in a well-ventilated place, adz headashedz, and

3

naudzea to avoid too much exrodzure. Avoid contact with mucus membranes such as the mouth, genitals, and euedz. Sitrudz oildz should be refrigerated adz they have a shelf-life of approximately one year. Edzdzential oildz angelica, sitrudz (including Bergamot), retitgrain and Saint John's wort can cause rhotodzendzitivitu. They also increase the risk of dzunburn even from moderate dzun exposure. Essential oils should not be used unless you are a trained rrorerlu in the proper way to dzafelu use them. They are powerful and can be toxic if used in excess.

Aromatherapy is a form alternative medicine that emrloudz rlants essential oils to support well-being and health. These oildz have a lot of health benefits, but they are still controversial. Indztagram feeddz and Pinterest boardsdz have been lauding thedze rlant derived extrastdz in recent years for their ability to do almost everything.

Essential oildz can play a pivotal role in rromoting well-being. Research has shown that essential oildz have powerful pharmacological properties. The online fervor robbed by enthudziadztis advertising samraigndz, multilevel marketing strategies has made determining when essential oildz are a good choice for your health and wellness, and when another treatment might be more appropriate more difficult.

Badzis need to be educated about udzing oils dzafelu or effestivelu, their uses, and how they can be safely integrated into everyday life. This'dz besaudze that edzdzential oils may be rowerful medisine or irresponsible. These are the essential facts to help you enjoy aromatherapy without exposing yourself to potential dangers.

Aromatherapy (aromatherapy) was originally defined as adz "the art of essential oildz." However, due to rapid development and the large amount of medical redzearsh devoted to aromatherapy research, it is now adz the "art", or "dzsiense", of aromatheraru. To be more precise, aromatheru refers to the art of extracting high-quality natural oils from flowers, leaves, roots, bark and other rartdz to enhance or redztore rdzushologisal or rhudzisal wellness. Aromatheraru is a specialty that allows peorle to use a wide range of essential oils to treat a variety of medical conditions.

This Thidz review will cover everything you need to know regarding edzdzential oilsdz and their effects on your health.

Chapter 1: Essential Oils Today

Enhance Your Physical Wellness

Absence of activity, horrible eating routines, and a bounty of ecological poisons are regular to the present current way of life. These variables would all be able to decrease vitality levels and leave the body feeling unequal. Fundamental oils and enhancements containing basic oils can give a portion of the arrangements expected to reestablish harmony in your life from purifying and weight the board to supporting each arrangement of the body.

Purify Your Home

You can likewise utilize fundamental oil-injected recipes you make yourself to clean your home. You can evade those dreadful compound equations and appreciate significant serenity when you clean your ledges, messy surfaces and mop up clingy meddles with the delicate yet compelling intensity of fundamental oils.

Refine Your Skin

Since forever, individuals have been utilizing basic oils to advance clear appearances, mellow the indications of maturing, and support solid hair. These serious hair and skin arrangements utilize just normal fixings and make it simple to appreciate the advantages of fundamental oils each day as you rediscover your common sparkle and cleanse all the synthetic compounds from your excellence schedules.

Create Deep Spiritual Awareness

Studies show that constituents in basic oils can invigorate olfactory (feeling of smell) receptors and animate the districts in the cerebrum related with feeling, memory, and perspective. You can upgrade your profound practice by weakening and applying certain basic oils legitimately to your feet, wrists, behind the ears, or by diffusing them in a tranquil space.

The Basics Of Essential Oils

How Essential Oils Are Made

Fundamental oils can be extricated either through refining or articulation.

The Practice Of Distillation

For refining the plant material is put on an opened rack inside a still. The still is fixed and, contingent on the strategy, water, steam, or a mix of the two gradually gets through the plant material and eliminates its oils. These oils ascend as a fume through an interfacing pipe that leads through a condenser. This condenser cools the rising fume once again into a fluid structure whereupon the fluid is then gathered in a compartment beneath the condenser. Since oil and water don't blend, these basic oils will be discovered coasting on the outside of the water which is then redirected.

The Practice of Expression

Articulation, otherwise called cold squeezing, is an extraction strategy that is principally utilized in handling citrus fundamental oils, for example, lemon, lime, bergamot, tangerine and sweet orange. During the extraction cycle, the skin of the natural product is set in a turning holder with spikes so as to penetrate the strip. After penetrating the skin delivers the fundamental oil which is then gathered in a little holder beneath the expresser.

Distilled Vs. Expressed Oils

Numerous fragrance based treatment organizations sell both communicated and refined citrus oils from similar types of plant. Refined citrus oils will break down significantly more rapidly and are shakier than their communicated partners. Along these lines, refined citrus oils are not suggested for fragrance based treatment use, with one special case. Refined lime basic oil is viewed as better in smell and impact than its communicated partner and is the prescribed oil to utilize.

Application of Essential Oils

Basic oils are commonly applied in one of three different ways: topically (applied on the skin), inward breath, or ingestion. Inside every one of these techniques, there are an assortment of ways for their utilization. For instance, in the event that you needed to apply a fundamental oil topically, you could utilize packs, showers, splashes, creams, gels, or back rub oils.

Which Application Method To Use

Pick your application technique dependent on the impact you want and the fundamental oil you are utilizing. Some fundamental oils are aggravations when utilized undiluted, so you may need to utilize those through inward breath or intensely weakened with transporter oils or water. In the event that you are uncertain about which application technique to utilize, counsel an accomplished aromatherapist.

Inhaling Essential Oils

Basic oils can be breathed in utilizing an assortment of methods and gadgets:

Diffuser: Essential oils are set in a diffuser gadget, with warmth or water so they dissipate.

Dry Evaporation: Several drops of basic oil are put on a cotton ball or tissue and permitted to dissipate into the air.

Steam: Drops of basic oil are added to a bowl of steaming water, which rapidly disintegrates the oil. You at that point place a towel over your head and over the bowl of water with fundamental oil drop(s) and inhale profoundly.

Spray: Drops of basic oils are set in a water-based arrangement, shaken, and showered into the air so as to aerate a room or set a mind-set.

Applying Essential Oils Topically

Basic oils can be applied to the skin utilizing an assortment of procedures, nonetheless, most basic oils must be weakened before applying straightforwardly to the skin. Here are different strategies for effective application:

Compress: The fundamental oil is weakened in a fluid transporter (water or oil) and applied to a dressing or legitimately to the influenced region. Discretionary warmth or cold can be applied.

Gargle: Drops of basic oil are added to water. You blend, at that point wash the arrangement and let it out. Try not to swallow it.

Bath: Drops of fundamental oils are added to shower water in a dispersant or in shower salts preceding stepping in. This strategy brings about retention through the skin, just as inward breath of the volatilized basic oil.

Massage: Drops of basic oil are added to a characteristic transporter oil and applied to skin territories with delicate scouring.

How to Dilute Essential Oils

Basic oils ought to be weakened in a transporter substance like coconut oil, vegetable oil, nut oil, or water at no more noteworthy fixation than 3%.

A 3% arrangement would be proportional to 1tsp. of transporter substance to 3 drops fundamental oil. For back rub or application over huge regions of the body, a 1% arrangement (one drop of basic oil in one tsp. of transporter substance) is commonly a protected fixation. Simply recall that in the event that you use water as a transporter, make certain to shake or blend your answer a long time before application.

Applying Essential Oils Internally

In the United States, the ingestion of basic oils is just suggested under the management of an authorized medical care supplier, be that as it may, fundamental oils can be applied inside in an assortment of ways, including oral ingestion and suppositories.

Chapter 2: What is Aromatherapy?

Aromatherapy: The Origins

What is Aromatherapy?

Aromatherapy, a holistic healing method that uses essential oils, is a holistic approach to healing. Essential oils, which are concentrated extracts of the leaves, seeds and roots of plants, have been used therapeutically for more than 6,000 years. Aromatherapy dates back to ancient Indian, Chinese and Egyptian cultures. They used essential oils for cosmetics, drugs, and hygienic, ritualistic and spiritual purposes.

Modern Aromatherapy: The Founding of Modern Aromatherapy

Rene-Maurice Gattefosse (a French chemist) coined the term "aromatherapy".

After a laboratory explosion, Rene-Maurice Gattefosse discovered the healing powers of lavender oil while treating a hand injury. Gattefosse, who founded aromatherapy in 1928, published many books on the subject. Jean Valnet was one of Gattefosse's followers. He used essential oils to treat wounds and skin infections among wounded soldiers during World War II.

What is Aromatherapy?

Researchers are still not sure exactly how aromatherapy works. Scientists believe our sense of smell could play a part. Some scientists believe essential oils molecules may interact with hormones and enzymes in the blood. Aromatherapy massage can be a great way to experience essential oils. It allows you to both smell and absorb the oils through your skin.

No matter how they work, we know that they do work. Many people have experienced amazing success stories with essential oils and aromatherapy.

Aromatherapy and Essential Oils

What are essential oils?

Essential oils are liquids that have been extracted from the stems and leaves of plants. Although they are called "oil", essential oils are not oily. Most are clear in color. Some oils, like orange, patchouli and lemongrass are yellow- or amber-colored.

Essential Oils Vs. Perfumes

Essential oils have chemical compositions that can be used to provide psychological and physical healing benefits. They are usually applied to the skin by inhalation.

Essential oils are not the same as perfume oils or fragrance oils. They are extracted from plants. Perfume oils, on the other hand, are synthetic fragrances or chemicals that have been artificially made. They do not provide the same therapeutic benefits as essential oils.

What are the uses of essential oils?

Essential oils are very concentrated and can be used in small amounts. You can use essential oils topically by mixing them with carrier oils like grapeseed oil, sweet almond oil, coconut oil, and apricot kernel oil. Then, apply the mixture to your skin to absorb or inhale.

Inhaling oil can be beneficial in certain situations. The oil molecules will enter your lungs and then be absorbed into your bloodstream.

Purchasing Essential Oils

Essential oils are sold in small quantities and may vary in quality and price. Price and quality can be affected by the rarity of the essential oil, its country of origin, climate conditions, distiller quality standards and how much oil it produces.

Essential oil blends can also be purchased. Blends of high-quality essential oils can be cheaper than buying individual essential oils. However, the downside is that you can't control the mix and you won't be able to mix it with other oils reliably because you don't know its exact composition.

An Overview of Essential Oils

The History of Essential Oils Around the World

Many cultures have used essential oils for centuries, also known as aromatic oils. They can be used for healing, religious or other purposes depending on their culture. Although we are unable to pinpoint when essential oils became popular as healing agents for the sick, the spread of knowledge about the benefits of essential oils has been remarkable.

Lascaux in France, which is in the Dordogne Region, was the first to show the healing powers of certain plants. The cave paintings found in this area indicate that plants were used in daily life to treat ailments. Carbon dating has been done on the area as far back 18,000 B.C.E.

Egypt

Evidence and recorded history have proven that early Egyptians used aromatic oils back in 4500 B.C.E. In their daily lives, they used aromatic oils, balsams and aromatic vinegar, scented trees, spices, resins, and scented barks. They made pastes, powders and oils from plants. They used fragrances for religious purposes as well, dedicating particular fragrances to specific deities and anointing statues using their chosen oil. Myrrh, Cedar and other aromatic oils were used in embalming. These oils can be found on mummies from Egypt.

China

Between 2697 and 2597 B.C.E, during the reigns of Huang Ti (the Yellow Emperor), one of the first books on essential oils was published in China. His book, "The Yellow Emperor's Book of Internal Medicine", contains many uses of aromatic oils. It is still considered useful by practitioners of eastern medicine.

India

In Indian medicine, aromatic oils have been used in healing potions and salves for over 3,000 years. There are over 700 herbs and spices listed in Indian medicine's written texts as healing agents, including sandalwood, ginger, cinnamon, myrrh, and sandalwood. Their medical methods, known as Ayur Veda were used to replace ineffective antibiotics during the Bubonic Plague or the 'Black Death'. Essential oils and aromatic plants were believed to be a part of the divine nature, and played an important role in traditional Ayurvedic medicine's spiritual and philosophical outlook.

Greece

Between 400 and 500 B.C.E. The Greeks began to document their knowledge of essential oils, mainly from the Egyptians. Hypocrites, the Greek physician and 'Father in Medicine', documented over 300 essential oils, including peppermint, saffron and thyme.

Rome

Romans are known for their use of perfumed oils on their clothing, bedding, and bodies. They used oils for massages and in baths. Roman doctors brought with them books written by Hypocrites during the fall of Rome's Empire. These texts were later translated into Arabic, Persian, and other languages.

Europe

Knights and their armies carried the knowledge of herbal remedies they had learned from the Middle East to Western Europe during the Crusades. In the hope of fighting the Bubonic Plague, people burned frankincense and pine in the streets. These areas have seen a decrease in the number of people who succumbed to plague.

Essential Oils Today

Improve Your Physical Well-being

Today's lifestyle is characterized by poor nutrition, inactivity, and a high level of environmental toxins. All of these factors can affect energy levels and cause imbalances in the body. Supplements containing essential oils and essential oils may provide the solution to balance your life, from weight management and cleansing to supporting all systems of the body.

Make Your Home a Purity

Essential oil-infused products you make can be used to clean your home. It's possible to avoid using harmful chemicals and have peace of mind when you clean your countertops, mop up sticky messes, and wipe down dirty surfaces with the gentle and effective power essential oils.

Get your skin reshape

Essential oils have been used for centuries to maintain healthy hair, improve skin complexions and soften the signs that come with aging. These natural products are safe for your skin and hair. You can enjoy the benefits of essential oils every single day, rediscovering your natural glow and eliminating all chemicals from your beauty routines.

Create Deep Spiritual Awareness

Research has shown that essential oils have the ability to stimulate the sense of smell (olfactory) receptors. They also stimulate brain regions associated with emotion, memory, mood, and state-of mind. Some essential oils can be used to enhance spiritual practice. You can either apply them directly to your feet or wrists behind your ears or diffuse them in a quiet area.

Chapter 3: Can Aromatherapy Reduce Anxiety?

Aromatherapy can be an effective tool to combat anxiety. Aromatherapy is an effective natural treatment to ease anxiety symptoms. To alleviate anxiety, essential oils and calming herbs may be used. These benefits can be used to improve your physical, spiritual and emotional well-being. It is possible to reduce anxiety by using essential oils regularly over time.

Anxiety sufferers can use aromatherapy in addition to a sugar-free and caffeine-free lifestyle. Regular exercise is also an option. Combining aromatherapy with these factors will increase your chances of having an anxiety-free life. It will also improve the feeling of calm.

Aromatherapy can be used to ease anxiety by helping one embrace their thoughts and feelings with comfort and softness. This involves the science of translating the smell of an oil to a positive idea of what it reminds us of. Your sense of smell can travel into the limbic brain, which is responsible for our emotions and memories.

Aromatherapy for anxiety can be used in the bath just as with stress. It is the easiest and best way to get it. An aromatherapy bath can be very relaxing. Numerous studies have shown that lavender aromatherapy can help relieve anxiety. These studies suggest that aromatherapy for anxiety could affect mood, cognitive performance, and relaxation. This information is still being confirmed by more studies.

Chapter 4: Recipes

Synopsis

Aromatherapy is a rewarding way to make your own essential oil blends. You can make blends for the pure aromatic pleasure or for use in your home as a room scent.

You can also make essential oil blends for therapeutic purposes, such as relieving aching muscles or reducing the incidence of acne.

"blahs" etc...

Recipes

Aromatherapy Bath Oil Recipe

* 2 ounces carrier oil such as Jojoba

* 20 drops of lilac Essential Oil, or 15-20 drops of your personal blend of essential

oils. (Make sure they are not skin irritating EOs).

Instructions: Combine the oils and keep in a glass container. You can double or triple the formula.

To Use: Don't use all 2 ounces of the bath oil in one tub. Once you have drained your bathwater, add approximately 1/4 ounce (8-8ml) of the bath oils blend to your water.

Blend the ingredients well and then get in. To ensure that essential oils don't evaporate before you enter the tub, it is best to add bath oil before the water boils.

This bath oil mixture is safer than adding pure essential oils directly to the water. Pure essential oils added to the bathwater can settle on one area of your skin, causing irritation.

Aromatherapy Bath Salts Recipe

* 3 C salt. You can choose from the following salt types: Dead Sea Salt or Himalayan Pink Salt. Salts come in many different sizes. Mixing different grain sizes can make salts look more appealing. Although chunkier salts look more appealing, larger salts can take longer to dissolve in the tub. It may also be more painful or difficult to sit or stand on salt chunks that aren't completely broken down.

* Take between 15 and 24 drops of the essential oil or essential oil mixture you have chosen. You should carefully read the safety data before you use any oil.

* Optional: Fractionated Coconut Oil, 1 TB JoJoba, or an additional carrier oil to moisturise.

Instructions

Combine the salt and water in a bowl. Add the oil to your salt mixture and mix well with a spoon, fork or a spoon. Then, add the essential oils you have chosen.

Mix the mixture again. Mix the mixture in a pretty container, such as a salt tube or jar. Make sure it has a tight fitting lid. Salts that are not kept in an airtight container will lose their fragrance more quickly.

You might want to make sure that you mix the oils well after a day.

You can color your salts!

You can leave your bath salts un-dyed for the best bath salt recipe. Some exotic salts, such as Black Sea Pink Salt and Hawaiian Red Sea Salt, are naturally colorful. These salts can be mixed with Dead Sea salt or plain sea salt to create a flecked effect.

You can add color to your salts with FD&C liquid dye, mica powder or essential oils. Mix FD&C grade liquid color well and only add a small amount at a time.

Mix mica powder in a small amount (1/16-1/8 teaspoon is usually enough) and only mix it well. Too much mica powder or dye can cause skin to turn yellow.

Use bath salts in a soft pastel shade. You must also ensure that your bath salts are safe for skin and that users of the mixture don't experience any allergies or sensitizations.

To utilize:

Add 1/2-1 cup salts to the running tub water. Mix well before adding the salts to the tub. You can add the bath salts to the tub right before you get in. This will prevent the essential oils from quickly vaporizing.

Instead of waiting for the water to boil,

Chapter 5: Using Aromatherapy

Purchasing Essential Oils

Many aromatherapists (and clients of aromatherapists) prefer that their essential oils contain no synthetic additives, especially if they will be applied to the skin and absorbed during massage. The federal government requires that some oils have a standard level of certain chemical/aromatic components. This is known as the Food Chemical Codex (FCC). One example is lemongrass essential oil- it must contain at least 75 percent aldehyde by law. lxiv The federal government does not prohibit the addition of synthetic chemicals to essential oils to meet their FCC; thus, "food grade" essential oils does not mean that they are all natural. lxv

Essential oils used in aromatherapy should be "therapeutic grade." However, there is no regulatory body in the United States that dictates the standards of a therapeutic grade essential oil- the standard is agreed upon by the industry. lxvi The terms "pure essential oil" and "aromatherapy oil" can also be misleading, or used to deceive customers. Also, avoid oils labeled "fragrance oil" or "perfume oil" because they contain synthetic additives. lxvii Do not rely on product labeling when purchasing an essential oil. Use the following guidelines, and ask the right questions of the vendor before making your purchase. lxviii

Never purchase essential oils sold in clear plastic containers. Light degrades essential oils. Also, chemicals in the plastic will leech into the oil over time, making it less pure and even possibly toxic.lxix Always purchase essential oils stored in dark glass bottles. lxx Likewise, avoid buying oils that have a rubber stopper because the oil can degrade the stopper. lxxi Use vendors that label the bottles with both the common and the Latin botanical name. There are several variations of many essential oils, so the Latin name will tell you which variation you are purchasing, and also shows that the vendor is knowledgeable and that you are probably getting undiluted oil. The label should also include the country of origin for the oil. lxxii

If you buy essential oils in a store, select a bottle that does not have dust settled on the lid. That is a sign that the bottle has been sitting out, and oils degrade over time. You will end up with a lower quality product.lxxiii Pay attention to the vendor's pricing structure. Rarer, more difficult to produce essential oils (such as rose oil or jasmine oil) can be very expensive. A vendor that prices all the oils at the same basic price is more often than not selling diluted or cut oils. lxxiv Also, organic essential oils are made from plants that were grown without chemical fertilizers or pesticides- these oils are superior to non-organic oils. The label should state if a product is organic. lxxv

When purchasing an essential oil in the store in person, it is essential to smell it before buying it. Over time, you will develop the ability to distinguish between a diluted or synthetic oil and an unadulterated oil. Pure oils have a fuller, deeper smell than synthetics. lxxvi When purchasing the oils online or through mail order, ask the company to send you a sample before you buy anything, so you can smell it first. lxxvii You can even ask the vendor to provide a gas chromatography test, which will show you the purity of the oil. lxxviii Finally, put a drop or two of the oil on a piece of paper. When the oil evaporates, there should be no greasy or oily spot left on the paper. If there is, the oil is synthetic or diluted. lxxix

Storing Essential Oils

Store essential oils in dark colored glass containers.lxxx If you have large volumes of the oil, you can use a lined aluminum container. lxxxi Plastic containers are usually clear, and the light that comes into contact with the oils will degrade them. Plastic can also leach potentially toxic chemicals into the substance it contains. lxxxii Keep the bottles away from heat sources and out of sunlight. lxxxiii

You should also keep the bottles away from sources of moisture. When you open the bottle, try not to touch the inside of the lid or the edge of the reducer. lxxxiv If you purchase a large quantity of the oil, decant small amounts into 4 ounce (or smaller) amber glass bottles to minimize the contact the oil has with oxygen. Always keep the lid on the bottle tightly to keep air from coming into contact with the oil. lxxxv

Storing the essential oil in the refrigerator will help extend its shelf life. Some oils can last several years. Citrus oils degrade faster than other oils. lxxxvi Some oils may solidify in the refrigerator, but it does not effect their quality. Simply leave them out to come to room temperature before use, and they should melt. lxxxvii Avoid using oils that are so old that their smell has altered. lxxxviii

How to Use Essential Oils

Aerial distribution is the process of putting essential oil aromas into the air to alter mood, well being, or to disinfect a space (as noted in Chapter One). The easiest way to achieve aerial distribution is to pour two cups of boiling water in a bowl, and then add no more than 10 drops of a non-irritating oil. The steam from the boiling water will distribute the oil throughout the air in the room. lxxxix You can also light a candle and let it burn long enough to form a pool of wax around the wick. Put out the candle, pour a drop of the oil into the wax pool, and then relight the candle. Use caution because essential oils are flammable. xc Another method involves placing drops of essential oil on a tray and placing that over a tea candle.

These heat-based methods work quickly to spread the aroma through the room, but heat has its drawbacks. It alters the chemical makeup of the oil, which can change the smell or make the aromatherapy less effective. xci Despite this, there are several commercial diffusers that use heat. Lamp ring diffusers consist of a terra cotta ring into which you pour the oil. The ring then goes on top of a light bulb, and the heat diffuses the scent.xcii Electric heat diffusers have an electric heating element and then a small fan that distributes the scent. xciii

Non-heated diffusers are preferable because they do not use heat that could alter or damage the chemical make-up of the oils. Also, they are safer in terms of fire prevention. xciv Fan diffusers that do not use heat are effective. The oil goes onto an absorbent pad or small tray in front of a fan. When the fan is on, it distributes the smell without the use of heat. xcv Essential oil nebulizers are also heat-free. They work by separating the oils into small particles, making them easier to absorb through the lungs. When combined with the lack of heat, nebulizers become one of the best methods of aerial distribution; however, some thicker oils cannot be used in nebulizers. xcvi The micro-fine particles of oil dispersed into the air by a nebulizer are suspended longer, so they have more time to come into contact with pathogens. xcvii

Direct inhalation is another method of administration of aromatherapy. The easiest way to do this is to hold an open bottle of essential oils 6 to 8 inches from your nose and fan the aroma toward you. Do not touch the opening of the bottle. xcviii You can also place three drops on your hands, spread the oil over your palms, and then hold your hands in front of your face while you breath deeply. If you have sensitive skin or are using a potent oil, dilute it with a carrier. xcix This may be an attractive method for facial or head massages, as a way to end with a calming feeling. Dab a few drops of diluted essential oils on your pulse points as an alternative to chemical-laden perfumes. c

The final method of administering aromatherapy is through the rectum, vagina or mouth. The NCBTMB prohibits massage therapists from touching the genitalia, and most states require a massage therapist to be a licensed colonic technician in order to touch the rectum. The administration of essential oils orally should be left to medical professionals. These methods are more common in France and Germany. ci Using potent essential oils on these sensitive areas can also cause damage to the mucous membranes or other severe reactions. cii

Perhaps one of the best ways to incorporate aromatherapy into a massage practice is through topical application. Essential oils are generally too strong for direct application to skin, so they should always be diluted with a carrier oil. Some examples include apricot kernel oil, grapeseed oil, and other vegetable based oils. ciii The aromatherapist can also blend two or more essential oils together to create a desired effect. When doing so, start with only 10-25 drops so you do not waste oil, and make sure each oil is not contraindicated against whatever you are trying to treat. civ

When used during reflexology massage, aromatherapy oils can be used to affect specific areas of the body. cv The molecular structure of the oils is small and they are fat soluble, so massaging oils into the affected area will result in fast absorption. cvi However, be careful to never diagnose a patient's illnesses, or claim that aromatherapy can cure their ailments. This is in accordance with the NCBTMB Standard of Practice and the Food and Drug Administration guidelines.

Massage therapists should also comply with the NCBTMB Standard of Practice by receiving consent before administering aromatherapy.

Examples

There are hundreds of essential oils, many of which have more than one use. Here are just a few examples of essential oils and their uses.

Allspice- warming, comforting, pairs well with other spicy aromatics cvii

Amber- antispasmodic, calming, balancing cviii

Basil- invigorating, eases muscle spasms, intestinal issues cix

Bergamot- relaxation, antiseptic, helps dry up blemishes on the skin cx

Carrot Seed- helps with dry skin, wrinkle reducer, muscle relaxant cxi

Cedar wood- promotes lung function and relaxation, purifies the skin cxii

Chamomile- relaxation of mind and muscles, soothes muscle aches cxiii

Cinnamon- one of the strongest anti-microbial essential oils, been in use for this reason for over 2,000 years cxiv

Clary Sage- eases muscular pain, relaxing, may assist with insomnia cxv

Clove- energizing, antimicrobial cxvi

Eucalyptus- boosts immune system, helps relieve respiratory discomfort, invigorating cxvii

Fennel- aids digestive system, firms cellulite, may help with milk production in post-partum women cxviii

Geranium- skin balancing, useful in hormone balancing, antidepressant, relaxationcxix

Ginger- helps improve joint mobility and reduce pain from arthritis cxx

Grapefruit- energizing, antiseptic- do not use 12 hours before skin exposure cxxi

Hyssop- respiratory problems, alertness, fights fatigue cxxii

Jasmine- soothing, relaxant, aphrodisiac, reduces scarring, eases skin irritation, post-partum depression cxxiii

Kanuka- pain relief, clears inflammation, skin tonic cxxiv

Lavender- relaxation, wound care, hormone balance, alleviate depression cxxv

Lemon- invigorating, mental focus, antiseptic cxxvi

Lemongrass- insect repellant, cleansing, invigorating cxxvii

Marjoram- calming, warming, relieves congestion, relieves muscle aches cxxviii

Myrrh- soothing for skin, helps relieved chapped skincxxix

Myrtle- "clarifying, cleansing" cxxx

Neroli- relaxing, confidence-building, relieves anxiety and soothes nerves cxxxi

Nutmeg- aids in digestion, promotes easy sleep cxxxii

Orange- relaxation and sleep aid, toxin elimination, stimulates immune system, helps with water retention cxxxiii

Oregano- stimulates digestion and circulation, relieves muscular aches and pains cxxxiv

Patchouli- soothing, moisturizes mature skin, dandruff prevention, do not use if you have insomnia cxxxv

Pepper, Black- helps with muscle suppleness, therefore useful for pre-athletic massages cxxxvi

Peppermint- helps relieve headaches cxxxvii

Rose Otto- one of the oldest essential oils, encourages creativity, cheering, used in skin creams cxxxviii

Rosemary- uplifting, stimulates immune system and digestive system, eases muscle tension cxxxix

Rosewood- antimicrobial, aphrodisiac, eases dry and oily skin cxl

Sage- eases disorders of digestive system, helps ease menstrual discomfort, regulates nervous system cxli

Sandalwood- treats dry hair or dry skin, aphrodisiac, body fragrance, blends well with other soothing aromatics cxlii

Tea Tree- anti-fungal, immune system booster cxliii

Thyme- can increase memory effectiveness and concentration, antidepressant, eases respiratory ailments cxliv

Valerian- grounding, soothing, promotes sleep cxlv

Ylang Ylang- relaxation, alleviation of depression cxlvi

One simple way to begin experimenting with aromatherapy is to select one of the more all-purpose essential oils and begin using it on yourself. Chamomile, lavender and rosemary are all relatively mild (and you can dilute them) and can be used to treat a number of conditions. Research which conditions the selected oil is indicated for, and when you experience those symptoms (it can be as simple as a mild headache or tiredness), place a few drops on a tissue and breath in the aroma.

Chapter 6: To be considered the

risks and precautions

Essential oils and aromatherapy products can be used safely for everyone if they are used correctly. Essential oils are extremely concentrated and should be used with caution.

Undiluted essential oils: Never apply undiluted essential oils directly to your skin unless you are in immediate danger. You can use it to treat cuts, burns, or bites. To soothe and prevent infection, a single drop of undiluted Chamomile Roman Oil, Chamomile Roman Oil or Tea Tree Oil can be applied. However, it is best to only use them once or twice. Tea Tree oil can cause allergic reactions in some people if applied to the skin repeatedly.

Undiluted essential oils should not be used on sensitive areas such as the eye, mouth and genitals. Unattended pets, children and polished surfaces should not be exposed to them. Undiluted oils should never be used on children younger than 3. Children under the age of 3 years have delicate and weaker internal organs that cannot effectively eliminate oils or manage metabolites.

Pregnancy: Before using essential oils, your doctor, midwife, or aromatherapist must be consulted. After your doctor gives their approval, essential oils should only be used in the first trimester. Then, only use them at a 1% concentration which is half of the normal strength.

To ensure that essential oils are safe for use during pregnancy, it is a good idea consult your supplier or aromatherapists. There are many misconceptions about which essential oils should not be used. Some aromatherapy books even list a large number of oils that may be contraindicated.

Many misinformations are based on internal plant use in herbal preparation. This is not the same thing as external application of diluted essential oils for massage. Many contraindicated essential oils can be used as food additives. Experts in essential oils argue that they cannot be considered to be dangerous.

It is best to avoid essential oils if you have had miscarriages in the past.

Avoid essential oils during pregnancy

Camphor

Rosemary

Sage

Savin Oil

Babies, infants, and young children: Essential oils should not be used on babies younger than 3 years. Essential oils should only be used in a fraction of their usual concentration. The correct method to determine the right amount of essential oil for a baby is to consider the infant's weight.

1 to 2 stone - 1 drop of essential oil

2 to 4 stones + 2 to 3 drops essential oils

4 to 6 stone - 4 to 5 drops essential oils

Internal Use: Essential oils should not be taken internally unless you have been trained in aromatherapy. This training is not common for aromatherapists, so make sure you check it out.

Although you may find articles and books praising the benefits of essential oils in your body, it is best to consult a professional before taking any steps.

Photosensitivity: Some essential oils can be photosensitive and should not be used before sunbathing. These are the main oils that cause skin to become photosensitive in aromatherapy:

Angelica Root Oil

Bergamot Oil Expressed

Bitter Orange Oil

Cumin Oil

Cold-Pressed Lemon Oil

Lime Oil Extracted

Targeted oil

Bergamot oil is a great oil to enjoy the sun.

Irritators and Sensitizers - Some essential oils can cause skin irritation if they are used in high quantities or for prolonged periods of time. These essential oils are the most well-known oils in this group.

Bay Leaf Oil

Cinnamon Bark Oil

Clove Oil (Stem, Leaf, Bud)

Lit sea Cubeb Aka May Chang Oil

Oregano Oil

Targeted oil

Thyme Oil White and Red

Essential oils that should be avoided: Certain essential oils should not ever be used in aromatherapy because of the risk of toxicity, severe irritation, sensitization, or other serious health hazards. Although most aromatherapy suppliers are not able to offer these oils, those listed below have been introduced to the market. They should only be used by people who have completed the required specialist training.

Parsley Herb Oil

Pennyroyal Oil

Savin Oil

Tansy Oil

Wintergreen Oil

Wormwood Oil

Flammability: Essential oils can be flammable. Do not use essential oils in direct sunlight or near any ignition source.

Safety precautions for aroma therapists

All essential oils should be kept out of reach from children and pets.

Photosensitizing essential oils should not be used before going to the sun. If photosensitizing essential oil were used to the skin, it is recommended that the client avoid the sun and tanning booth for at most twenty-four hours.

You should not use the same essential oil for too long. It can cause skin irritation and sensitization.

Do not use essential oils that you don't know anything about. Before you apply it to yourself or others, research the oil.

Avoid using undiluted essential oils on your skin, unless indicated otherwise.

It is a good idea to test the skin for any potential sensitivities or allergies that your client might have.

Learn the safety data for each essential oil, and understand the context of its use.

Be cautious when you treat a woman who is pregnant or trying to get pregnant.

Keep essential oils out of the eyes.

Essential oils can be extremely inflammable and should not come into direct contact with flames like candles, fire, matches or cigarettes.

Good ventilation is essential in a treatment room.

If you are not properly trained, do not use essential oils internally.

For beginners, aromatherapy tips

You can find many tips and tricks from different sources. I have listed some here for your convenience.

Do not:

Do not buy perfume oils thinking that they are the same as essential oils. Essential oils are not offered by perfume oils. Essential oils can be used in aromatherapy to provide therapeutic benefits, even if they are not intended for use in your daily life. These benefits are not associated with perfume oils.

Essential oils should not be purchased with rubber dropper caps. Essential oils can be very concentrated, and the rubber will become a gum, ruining the oil.

Avoid buying oils from vendors at street markets, craft shows, and other events that are limited in time. Many vendors realize that novices have limited resources and may not be able to pay them back later. Although there are many highly-respected sellers at these events, this caution is for novices who may not be able to judge quality.

Do it:

Learn as much about aromatherapy as possible. Although it is easy to start aromatherapy, there are many safety issues you should be aware of. It would be wise to continue reading about essential oil safety.

You should be careful about where your essential oils are purchased. There are many factors that can affect the quality of essential oils. Some companies might falsely claim their oils are pure or undiluted, but they are not.

When shopping for oils, learn how to compare apples with apples. Anise, Bay, Cedarwood, Eucalyptus, and Lavender are some of the common names for essential oils. Each of these plants can be grown in different ways. The botanical name, also known as its Latin name, is used to distinguish these varieties from other plants. As well as the differences in the properties and the aromas of different oils, so does their general cost. Therefore, it is important to pay close attention to the names of the botanical ingredients. The common botanical names of the two oils in Bay are Pimenta Racemosa and Laurus Nobilis.

It is important to identify the country of origin of the oil. Essential oil sellers who are good will provide the country of origin and botanical names for all oils they sell. Also, make sure to compare oil from different companies.

You may be able to purchase oils from well-respected mail-order companies, which can result in higher quality oils for a lower price. There is often a wide variation in the quality of oils between companies and stores.

Your oil should be stored in dark glass (cobalt or amber) and kept dry. To store essential oils, you can use wooden boxes and wooden floppy disk holders.

You should pay particular attention to safety information regarding essential oils you use. If you are pregnant or have any medical conditions, this is even more important.

Do not forget to include aromatherapy in your life.

FAQs

You will have many questions about aromatherapy as a beginner. Although it is best to consult an aromatherapist, there are still many questions you might have about how to start your introduction to aromatherapy, what the differences between essential oils, perfumes, and other topics.

Although I have provided some helpful tips in the section before, I have listed below some important questions you should ask yourself before you begin your journey into aromatherapy. These questions will help you get an idea of what information you will need before you start your journey into aromatherapy. For any additional questions, consult an aromatherapist.

What essential oils are the same as perfumes?

It is important not to confuse essential oils with fragrance oils or perfumes. Essential oils are naturally produced by plants, while fragrance oils are chemically manufactured to imitate certain aromas in perfumes, colognes and candles.

Are essential oils able to be applied directly to the skin?

It is not recommended. Essential oils in their purest form can cause skin irritation. Some oils may even penetrate the bloodstream and pass through the skin. Mixing essential oils with carrier oils or a base oil can reduce the risk of skin irritation.

What are the benefits of essential oils?

Essential oils should not be used internally. Essential oils can be toxic if they are swallowed due to their high concentrations.

How do you apply essential oils best?

The way you apply essential oils can have an impact on their healing properties. The oils will deliver a better result when used in small quantities, either with water or with a carrier or massage oil.

Can I use essential oil if I'm pregnant?

Yes, but be careful. It is best to avoid essential oils in the first trimester. Then, use them sparingly (no more that 1% dilution) until the end of the pregnancy. Essential oils such as grapefruit, grapefruit and mandarin are safe to use in pregnancy.

How do I store my essential oils?

It is best to keep essential oils in dark glass bottles with screw caps. Essential oils should be kept dry and out of direct sunlight.

How can I find out what essential oils do for different parts of my body?

Some essential oils can have an emotional or physical effect by themselves. Peppermint, for example, is known to be a mood-lifter and lavender, a calming oil. Blending oils with other oils can achieve the desired psychological or physiological effect. For example, ylang-ylang can be combined with grapefruit to reduce stress. Each essential oil offers its own unique benefits.

What aromatherapy can do for you?

Aromatherapy is often referred to as aromatherapy. However, essential oils are intended to be absorbed through the skin, massage, the lungs and inhalation. Aromatherapy can be used to reduce stress and to detoxify, rejuvenate, and cleanse the body. Aromatherapy can also be used to treat many other conditions.

What are the best precautions to take during therapy?

Essential oils can cause skin reactions, so it is important to be cautious about the quality of essential oils. Some people experience skin irritation due to overuse of essential oils. Others have adverse reactions when the oils are applied. Incorrectly using oils or taking them internally can cause more severe reactions. People with epilepsy or high blood pressure should not attempt to treat their condition. Young children and pregnant women need to be extra cautious.

What are the potential risks of Aromatherapy?

If essential oils are taken internally, they can prove to be extremely toxic. Externally applied oils can also have unintended effects, such as causing uterine contractions during pregnancy. It is important to not overestimate oils' healing abilities. If you are in a serious situation, a physician should be consulted.

What are the benefits of aromatherapy?

Many gift shops have begun to market scented candles, potpourri and pomanders as "Aromatherapy". However, true treatments rely on essential oils from healing herbs. These oils are usually obtained by steam distillation or cold press from plants, flowers and leaves, as well as bark, bark, rind, and roots. These volatile and flammable oils can then be mixed with a carrier oil, which is usually vegetable oil like soy, evening primrose or almond oil. The oil is then applied to the skin, sprayed on the skin, inhaled, or vaporized. While one can seek treatment under the guidance of an aromatherapist certified in aromatherapy, many people use the oil for their own home remedies. There is not much agreement about issues like the right amount of oil to achieve the desired effect, how to administer it, and how long to keep the treatment going.

What does essential oil do for the skin?

Essential oils can have a profound effect on the activity of the capillaries, and the vitality of the tissues, when applied to the skin. Their application can quickly repair various tissues.

Chapter 7: Lavender

Lavender is among the most widely studied essential oils you can find out there today. According to one study carried out on Lavender oil, lavender oil aromatherapy can help you reduce blood pressure, heart rate and body temperature. It has also been found to be effective for changing the brain waves to a far more relaxed state, which is why it is so effective when dealing with high stress levels and anxiety disorders.

Lavender is also quite effective for improving the quality of your sleep and for the treatment of mild to chronic insomnia. It is also helpful in treating depression and anxiety in women, reduction of post traumatic stress in patients after major surgeries and other serious medical conditions.

Lavender essential oil's unique scent is also known to help stimulate brain pathways, which include your limbic system, which is connected directly to your memories and emotional response.

The use of lavender for aromatherapy is considered safe generally, except if you have any history of lavender allergy.

How to Use:

Apply 2-4 drops directly to the affected areas and massage or diffuse for 1 hour 3 times per day.

Yuzu

Yuzu is a yellow citrus fruit mostly found in East Asian countries and often used in the preparation of Asian cuisines.

According to one new study from a group of Japanese researchers, Yuzu citrus scent can be very soothing for anxiety and stress conditions as well as for lowering your heart rate within 15 minutes, with the effects lasting for as long as half an hour or more.

The Japanese have a long custom of yuzu baths in which whole yuzus float in very hot baths to help with stress relief. As an alternative to yuzu, you can use other citrus fruit essential oils such as lemon, which has been found to help stimulate and increase heart rates.

How to Use:

Apply 1 drop of lemon essential oil mixed with 1 tablespoon of olive oil, massage deeply and thoroughly. Also you can diffuse 2-3 drops of lemon or Yuzu for 1 hour about 3 times daily.

Bergamot

Citrus bergamot is the source of the bergamot essential oil. Italian folk medicine has been using this essential oil for ages. However, there are new studies that suggest this essential oil can relieve anxiety, tension and stress. Bergamot essential oil is mostly used in fragrances, food flavoring, etc. It is also believed to have some great antibacterial properties.

Several clinical studies have shown that use of bergamot essential oil in aromatherapy helps reduce blood pressure, stress and heart rate. Some recent studies have also shown that bergamot can reduce severe pain.

How to Use:

Blend 5 drops of bergamot essential oil with 5 drops of lavender in 4 ounces of any carrier oil such as Sweet Almond, Avocado or olive oil. Use the blend to massage your hands, feet and legs to relieve stress.

Ylang Ylang

This essential oil has a sweet floral aromatic scent and is from Southeast Asia. Ylang Ylang scent has very relaxing effects and can help reduce your blood pressure according to studies. One study has also found that the scent of Ylang Ylang is effective for calming the nervous system, which can lead to reduced blood pressure and heart rates.

How to Use:

Mix 2 drops of ylang ylang with 1 tablespoon of coconut oil or sweet Almond oil, apply to desired area and massage for stress and depression relief.

Mix 2-4 drops of ylang ylang with few drops of bergamot essential oil, diffuse into your environment to relieve stress, tension, depression, anxiety, palpitation, etc.

Clary Sage

The Clary sage essential oil is extracted from the clary sage herb, known to be a very close relative of the common garden herb sage. Clary sage helps people going through some painful dental procedures such as tooth extraction to relax. Aromatherapy using clary sage oil has also been found to have anti-depressant effects.

How to Use:

Here are some ways to use the Clary Sage to get different results:

Rub 3-5 drops on the abdomen to ease menstrual cramps and other stomach discomforts.

Apply to pulse or feet to help balance hormones

Diffuse or apply to pillow at night to enhance restful sleep

Add to your bath water for a stress-relieving effect

Jasmine

Jasmine has a very sweet aroma and can be a very relaxing fragrance. Though less studied than most of the essential oils mentioned above, there are results that show jasmine aromatherapy can provide very calming effects.

How to Use:

Jasmine is believed to be in a class of its own among essential oils used in aromatherapy and can be used for different purposes and in different ways. Here are some examples of how to use your Jasmine essential oil:

Apply 2-3 drops to the desired area or mix with a neutral lotion and massage deeply.

Diffuse this relaxing essential oil in the evening for unwinding after a hectic day.

Include 5-10 drops in your evening warm bath for its calming, spa-like effects.

Orange

Orange and sweet orange essential oils are gotten from the rind of the orange fruit and have been linked to stress relief. According to one Brazilian study, those who inhaled sweet orange essential oil reported great improvement in their anxiety symptoms.

How to Use:

Apply 1 drop of orange mixed with 1-2 drops of olive oil and apply to the desired area. Alternatively, diffuse for 1 hour 3-4 times daily.

Rosemary

Rosemary is a common herb used in the kitchen. The herb is easily recognized by its woody scent. The aroma of this essential oil can soothe mental and emotional strain by reducing the activities of the hormones responsible for these conditions and their symptoms.

How to Use:

Add a few drops of Rosemary to your bath at night.

Peppermint

If you need a natural morning boot without a rooster or caffeine, you can use the peppermint essential oil to wake up your mind, senses and body to stay alert and face the day.

How to Use:

Dilute one drop of peppermint with 4 drops of olive oil, apply to desired area as required or diffuse aromatically for 10 minutes 3 times per day.

Frankincense

Frankincense is one of the gifts given to Jesus by the 3 wise men in the Bible, but today, it is known for its far-reaching healing and therapeutic properties. This essential oil has a variety of benefits such as inflammation reduction, pain relief, and stress and anxiety relief.

How to Use:

Diffuse 2-4 drops up to 1 hour 3 times per day.

The above are some of the common essential oils used. As mentioned earlier, it is important to dilute the essential oil with carrier oil. Let us learn more about carrier oils in the following chapter.

Carrier Oils: What Are They?

Before you can use essential oils in aromatherapy, these oils must be diluted in other oils known as carrier oils. This is because using them undiluted makes them too powerful and can lead to unwanted effects on your skin. While there are certain base lotions, you can use to dilute your essential oils, these carrier oils are the most ideal for diluting essential oils due to their versatile nature.

These carrier oils are known to provide the needed lubrication to allow your hands move freely all over your skin. It is preferable if the carrier oil has little or no odor.

Chapter 8: Recipes For Beauty

Aromatherapy Acne Recipe

Acne products that are commercially available are sometimes harsh on the skin due to the few amounts of chemicals in them. Creating a remedy for acne out of essential oils is a natural alternative.

You will need a clean bottle, preferably one made of amber glass. For the ideal essential oil blend, you will need 1 fluid ounce of either Jojoba essential oil or fractionated coconut oil, 6 drops of lavender essential oil, 5 drops of tea tree or manuka (also known as New Zealand tea tree) essential oil and a drop of geranium essential oil. Pour the selected carrier oil, jojoba or fractionated coconut oil, into the bottle then add the drops of essential oil needed. Roll the bottle gently for two minutes to allow the essential oils to mix. Repeat this rolling each time before using. To use, apply a small amount to the face and neck and areas with acne, avoiding the lips, eyes, nostril and the inside of your ears.

Aromatherapy Bath Oil Recipe

While some people prefer applying pure essential oil drops directly to bath water instead of concocting a bath oil following a bath oil recipe, there are in fact disadvantages. Essential oils do not mix well with water. There is a tendency therefore for the essential oil to settle on just one part of your skin. This might make your skin sensitive to the oil, causing bad reactions. A bath oil recipe using essential oils is a better option as this recipe will use essential oils diluted by a carrier oil to minimize the risk of sensitization. Carrier oils also provide additional moisture to your skin.

You will need two fluid ounces of Jojoba as carrier oil or any other carrier oil of your choice. Then, you will need twenty drops of lavender OR fifteen to twenty drops of your own blend of essential oils. All you have to do is blend all the ingredients together and store in a glass jar or glass bottle.

When taking a bath, use only around a quarter of the solution or about 8 milliliters on your bath water. It is best to pour the bath oil right before getting into the tub since essential oils tend to evaporate quickly.

Aromatherapy Bath Salts Recipe

For the ingredients, you will need three cups of bath salts of your choice. Recommended ones are Dead Sea Salts.

Salts from the Dead Sea are known to have high levels of Magnesium that is ideal for slowing skin aging and calming the nervous system. It also contains potassium which helps balance the moisture in your skin. You may also combine Dead Sea salt with other kinds of salt like Himalayan Pink Salt. You will also need 15-24 drops of the essential oil or blend of essential oils of your choice. For additional moisture, add a tablespoon of Jojoba or Fractionated Coconut Oil as carrier oil.

Mix the salts with the carrier oil in a large bowl with a fork. Then, add the drops of your chosen essential oil or essential oil blend. Mix everything together well. Transfer the mixture into a jar or salt tube, preferable airtight containers to preserve the aroma of the salts.

When taking a bath, use only around half a cup to a full cup of the mixed salts. It is best to pour the bath salts right before getting into the tub since essential oils tend to evaporate quickly. Make sure they are well dissolved in the water before getting into the tub for a comfortable bath.

Aromatherapy Body Power Recipe

For the container, a four-ounce body powder sifter will suffice. For the ingredients, the only things you will need are four ounces of arrowroot powder or an organic non-GMO cornstarch and 30 drops of lavender essential oil. If you have oily skin, a better alternative to arrowroot powder is up to half an ounce of white kaolin powder for oil absorption.

Pour the arrowroot powder or cornstarch or white kaolin to a mixing powder. Add the lavender essential oil then mix well together. Pour the powder mixture into the sifter bottle. Apply like an ordinary body powder, and avoid the sensitive areas of the body.

Aromatherapy Exfoliating Sugar Scrub Recipe

This exfoliating scrub recipe will help eliminate dead skin cells from your skin and is a good natural alternative to chemical-based commercial products that can irritate the skin easily.

You will need 8 ounces of Turbinado Sugar or Dermera Sugar. For the vegetable oil, you will need a fluid ounce of any of the following: Jojoba Oil, Watermelon Seed Oil, or Fractionated Coconut Oil. You will need one fluid ounce of vegetable glycerin and a fluid ounce of liquid Castile soap, half a teaspoon of Vitamin E oil, and a quarter teaspoon of an essential oil. Patchouli Essential Oil is recommended. You may opt to add a few drops of Spearmint Essential Oil. Place the sugar in a bowl, add the glycerin, vitamin E oil, and castile soap, then mix well with the soap. Add the essential oils then mix again.

Aromatherapy Hair Conditioner Recipe

For a natural alternative to commercially available hair conditioners, all you will need are a tablespoon of Jojoba and three drops rosemary essential oil for one application. Rosemary is not just good for hair care; it is also an alternative remedy for dandruff. Simply mix the Jojoba and the Rosemary Essential Oil in a small bowl.

When taking a bath, wet the hair with warm water before applying the blend. Leave the conditioner on for fifteen to thirty minutes for better results.

Aromatherapy Lotion Recipe

This recipe is very easy to follow for beginners. You would need eight fluid ounces of unscented hand or body lotion, preferably "lotion bases" from aromatherapy stores or natural product sellers. Pour the lotion or lotion base into a bowl. For the essential oil blend, you will need ten drops of patchouli essential oil, twenty drops of sandalwood essential oil, and five drops of carrot seed essential oil. These three essential oils are known to be god for dry skin. Add the lotions into the bowl and mix the mixture well. Pour the lotion mixture back into the bottle.

Aromatherapy Simple Perfume Recipe

For a simple version of a natural perfume, you will need nine drops of sandalwood, three drops of a choice among rose essential oil, jasmine essential oil or neroli essential oil. Rose essential oil has a floral and fruity scent. Jasmine absolute has a warm, floral and exotic aroma. Neroli essential oil has an intensely floral, citrusy, sweet and exotic smell. You will also need a tablespoon of jojoba. Mix and blend all the oils together well and store in an air-tight glass container. Dab a small amount into your pulse points and other areas you dab perfume into.

Aromatherapy Natural Perfume Recipe for Customizing

This is a core perfume recipe that you can use to create your own solid scent depending on your preference, personality or mood. For the ingredients, you will need 1/8 ounce of beeswax or floral wax. Using wax instead of a butter like shea butter makes the solution more rigid and stable, lessening the chances of melting in hot temperatures. Floral wax is a more organic, more vegan alternative to beeswax. Examples include rose wax, jasmine wax and mimosa wax. In addition to the wax, you will need half an ounce of Jojoba and 7 drops of the essential oil of your choice. Refer to the essential oil index in the previous chapter for a guide to selecting the type of aroma you might like. Instead of using one essential oil, you can also opt to use an essential oil blend.

To create the natural solid perfume, melt the wax and the jojoba together using a double boiler. Remove the mixture from heat when completely melted and allow it to cool but be careful not to let it turn solid. Add the essential oil or essential oil blend of your choice. Stir well. Pour the mixture into a container, preferable a jar. Allow the container to cool and the mixture to harden completely.

Aromatherapy Shampoo Recipe

This is a recipe that is easy to follow for beginners. For the container, a bottle with a capacity of eight ounces is preferable. You will need about seven fluid ounces of unscented shampoo base, preferably the ones available at natural products sellers or aromatherapy stores. You will also need a tablespoon of Jojoba for extra hydration for the hair. For the essential oils, you will need forty drops of Lavender essential oil, ten drops of rosemary oil, and five drops of ylang ylang oil.

Pour the unscented shampoo base into a bowl then add the essential oils. Mix everything together well. Pour the mixture into the eight-ounce bottle and voila! Aromatherapy shampoo in just three easy steps!

Aromatherapy Stretch Mark Recipe

When women go through pregnancy or when people lose weight, they sometimes fail to tend to their skin's needs, especially, moisture. Hence, they tend to develop stretch marks. Stretch marks can be a bit stubborn to eliminate. This recipe provides an alternative remedy to stretch marks using aromatherapy essential oils.

For the container, a four-ounce jar with an airtight lid will suffice. For the ingredients, you will need three ounces of cocoa butter, preferably deodorized. Cocoa butter that has not been deodorized tends to have a very strong scent that will not integrate well with the aroma you will produce in this recipe; also, a fluid ounce of avocado oil as your carrier oil. You can substitute with other carrier oils of your choice. For the essential oil, you will need four drops of neroli essential oil.

Melt the cocoa butter using a double boiler, add the avocado oil. Stir well. Transfer the mixture carefully into a small bowl and allow it to cool for around two minutes before adding the essential oil. This will prevent the essential oil from evaporating quickly when exposed to hot temperatures. Add in the neroli essential oil then mix. Pour the mixture into the jar.

This mixture is safe to able on the thighs and abdomen to reduce stretch marks. Application can be as frequent as twice a day. Immediately discontinue use of this mixture if irritation or sensitivity occurs.

Aromatherapy Facial Toner Recipe

For the container, you will need a bottle with a capacity of four ounces. You will need a fluid ounce of High Proof Vodka to help the oils be emulsified for a longer time. You will also need two and a half fluid ounces of Witch Hazel Hydrosol, eight drops of Grapefruit Oil, four drops of Tea Tree Oil and four drops of Cypress Oil. Grapefruit Essential Oil is known for aiding dull skin, Cypress Oil and Tea Tree Oil is both good for oily skin. Tea Tree Oil is also a known remedy for acne. If you prefer to leave the Vodka out, increase the amount of Witch Hazel Hydrosol.

Pour all the ingredients into the four-ounce bottle. Shake well to mix all the oils together. Shake well before each use. Apply to the face using a cotton ball.

Aromatherapy Cologne Recipe for Men

You will need two and a half fluid ounces of High Proof Vodka or Perfumer's Alcohol, a fluid ounce of distilled water. For the essential oils, you will need 15 drops of either Bergamot or Mandarin. You will also need 15 drops of Patchouli. You will also need five drops of Bay Laurel, either five drops of Oakmoss Absolute or two three drops of Vetiver, and three drops of Black Pepper or Hinger. You may add a drop to a couple of drops of Neroli.

Add the alcohol and water and place them in a sterile glass spray bottle, one that can contain around four ounces of liquid. Then, add the oils. Shake all the ingredients together. For the scent to blend properly, allow to mixture to rest for around five to six days, shaking the bottle one to two times a day.

Aromatherapy Mouthwash Recipe

This recipe will create a natural minty mouthwash as an alternative to commercial mouthwash products that contain too much flavorings. For the container, an eight-ounce bottle will suffice. You will need six fluid ounces of water and one to two fluid ounces of vodka. You may opt to substitute water for vodka, but take note that vodka helps kill germs and keep essential oils emulsified. For the essential oils, you will need eight drops of peppermint or spearmint essential oil, and five drops of myrrh.

Combine the water and vodka in the bottle. Add the essential oils, then shake well. Tighten the cap. Shake well before each use as essential oils do not stay mixed with water solutions.

Aromatherapy Shoe Deodorizer Recipe

For an aromatherapy version of a shoe deodorizer, you will need four tablespoons of baking soda, four tablespoons of non-GMC cornstarch, and five to six drops of lavender essential oil. In addition to minimizing shoe odor, lavender is also known as a remedy for athlete's foot.

Pour the baking soda and cornstarch in a bowl and mix together. Add the essential oils in a gradual manner. Stir well then store in an airtight container.

To use, sprinkle the mixture into the shoes at night. Before wearing the shoes, tap the soles to eliminate excess powder from the inside. Shoe odor will gradually lessen.

Aromatherapy Shower Gel Recipe

This is a very easy recipe to follow for beginners as it will not involve making a shower gel from scratch. Instead, this recipe calls for incorporating the ideal essential oils into a shower gel base. You will need a bottle with a capacity of containing around eight ounces of liquid. For the ingredients, you will need 7 fluid ounces of an unscented shower gel base, preferably the ones sold by aromatherapy stores or sellers of natural products. For the essential oils, you will need seventy drops of lavender essential oil or you can replace lavender with your favorite essential oil blend as long as you perform a skin patch test first.

Mix the unscented shower gel base and the essential oils in a bowl and blend them together. Mix well. Afterwards, transfer the mixture to the eight-ounce bottle using a funnel.

Chapter 9: Aromatherapy and Yoga

Perhaps you have used aromatherapy in your yoga classes. Maybe you have been to a spa or yoga studio that smells sweet, or perhaps your instructor uses incense sticks for final relaxation. Or maybe you had sore muscles from asana practice and needed a massage with essential oils to relax them. Aromatherapy can be used in yoga classes to enhance your awareness of your body and mind.

In the past, yoga and aromatherapy were closely linked. Attars (perfume made from plant material and a sandalwood base) are an integral part of Yoga practice in India. They help to relax the mind and increase relaxation. To massage the muscles, oils were used before asana practice.

Aromatherapy is an ancient holistic practice that offers physical, mental and spiritual relief. It is similar to yoga. Aromas can also be linked to memory and emotions, so emotions that are attached to our memories are immediately recalled. Similar to yoga, our bodies form the memories of a pose and these are woven into our cells. Our bodies remember the poses and go into a relaxed state every time we do a yoga posture. A longer hold on a pose can lead to healing. To enhance these associations and memories, aromatherapy can be added to the equation. You may also experience the same emotions and calming effects if essential oils are inhaled during yoga practice.

What can aromatherapy do to enhance yoga?

Aromatherapy oils are potent. It is best to use them under the supervision of a qualified aromatherapist or yoga teacher who is certified in aromatherapy. Reblended oils can be purchased with instructions on how to use them in yoga practice, and which oils are best for what aspects. Lemongrass is a great option if you want to boost your energy levels. Yoga can also be combined with lavender oil to help relax the mind and body.

There are some practicalities to consider when practicing yoga with aromatherapy (or Yogaroma). Essential oils can be made suitable for yoga practice in a variety of ways. This creates a calming effect, and allows for a small amount to be distributed throughout the room.

Aromatherapy blends can also be used to enhance your yoga practice. You should not apply a single essential oil to the skin. Instead, blend them or dilute them in carrier oil. It is possible to use "Yogaroma", a special blend that can be applied with a rolling ball tip to your pulse point (wrist behind the ears, third eye), and it is safer and more practical.

You can apply the oils to your pulse point at any hour of the day. You can also use oils from the mat to remind yourself of the blissful feeling you have during practice.

What role does essential oils play in Yoga?

Because of their effects on the body and chakras, essential oils can be used in different asanas.

Rose Absolute Oil can be diffused with oil burners in the bridge or backbends to increase their heart opening, particularly during times of grief and stress.

Sandalwood oil can be used in standing and warrior poses as a grounding oil.

Balancing and relaxing lavender oils can help promote calm surrender in standing and seated forward bends.

Peppermint oil may be used to invigorate postures like the downward facing dog or inversion. This oil is known for its ability to quickly energize both body and mind.

Clary Sage oil can be used for relaxation and to ease tension during twists. These massages work on the organs.

To maintain a clear mind and focus, apply a few drops of Peppermint or Frankincense oil to your forehead and chest. Inhale while inwardly posing. You can also experiment with your favorite poses and discover your favorites.

You can also use essential oils to clean your mat in an environmentally friendly manner. The mat will not only be sterilized, but it will also be scented. Different blends can have different effects. One blend may be more energizing than another. This can be altered to fit your yoga style and mood. You can make it even more interesting by adding essential oils like rosemary and tea tree to a spray bottle water.

Peppermint oil can be used to cool and refresh feet and bodies.

Essential oils can be applied to the pressure points and chakras.

To ease stress, massage oils like Eucalyptus or rosemary can be used.

For calming settings, you can light candles made from pure essential oils during a yoga class.

Sprays can be used in place of diffusers to provide an instant boost.

There are essential oils that can be combined with aromatherapy to support yoga practice. These oils are called Sacred Oils. These oils are precious and rare, and they have been used in rituals for thousands of years. These oils can be used to improve our yoga practice, to ground us, and to open our crown, third, and heart chakras.

Yogaroma uses three main sacred oils: Myrrh, Sandalwood, and Frankincense. Rose and Palo Santo Oils are also available.

Frankincense Oil: This oil can be used to ground the breath and open the upper chakras. This oil is excellent for meditation and following the breath. It is used often as a spiritual tool in ritual, prayer and meditation. It is a powerful, intoxicating scent that has many healing properties.

Sandalwood Oil: This essential oil has immediate effects and is one of the most effective. Sandalwood essential oil has a calming, cooling, and uplifting effect. Sandalwood oil can be applied to the temples and third eye points to promote calmness during meditation, relaxation after a stressful day, or to recharge your brain when you have more work to do. Sandalwood oil can be applied directly to the skin.

Myrrh Essential oil: The oil's aroma is uplifting, and it aids in spiritual opening. Myrrh has a mild and soothing effect on the central nervous systems, which can instill deep peace of mind. Myrrh strengthens our connection between the crown and base chakras. Myrrh is believed to reduce grief and heal emotional wounds, bringing peace and calm.

Rose oil is expensive, but it is worth the investment. Avoid synthetics. Rose oil can be applied to the throat, heart, or third eye center to deepen meditation, calm and cool an over-active mind, and creates feelings of love and compassion.

Palo Santo Oil can be used in conjunction with pranayama. This essential oil has a powerful, uplifting effect. This essential oil is useful for meditation, creativity enhancement, and tasks that require sustained concentration.

How does it feel to use Yogaroma oils in your practice?

Imagine yourself walking into your yoga class, surrounded by beautiful mats and fresh-cleaned blocks and straps. Silk eye masks, silk eye masks, and straps are all waiting for you. The room is filled with a wonderful aroma, the smell of burning wood filling the air. You place yourself on top of your mat and begin to practice. You will feel the soothing aromas in your lungs as you move and practice yoga.

Chapter 10: Skin Care And Aromatherapy

Skin not only covers and protects the body organs, it also excrets various toxins from the body through sweat and perspiration and, for the latter activity, skin pores serve as outlets for exit of toxins. If skin is healthy, good looking, soft, glazed, it is a boon for every one, whereas a rough skin denotes lack of sebacious oils that feed and nutrient the skin. Essential oils have excellent penetrative properties, apart from making useful moisturisers. But all essential oils and their preparations do not suit all types of skin. These oils can stimulate circulation of blood and the lymphatic system, cleanse the tissues which cause sluggishness to skin, treat various skin problems and general skin care.

Healthy skin is dependent on many factors, such as balanced diet, consisting of grain cereals, pulses, green vegetables, fresh seasonal fruits— rich in vitamins, minerals, dairy, poultry and sea products. It is pointed out that skin condition is also governed by various pshychic, emotional and sentimental factors. Environmental factors, pollutions in air & water, local weather conditions also play an important role in this regard.

Types of Skin

Certain weather conditions impact the skin greatly. For instance, skin can be dry in cold snowy and winter conditions, complexion usually darkens in summer, more oily during the period, in most conditions skin is more sticky and gives out unpleasant smell. It usually changes from puberty to menopause. So, one oil cannot be used for all the skins, rather it has to be changed in consonance with weather condition and the type of skin one has. Even oily skin can turn rough, cracked and dry and vice versa. Hence, choose an oil that suits your type of skin best.

Following classifications will give an idea about the properties that a particular oil possess.

Oils for Dry Skin

Chamomile, Geranium, Hyssop, Lavender, Patchouli, Rose, Sandalwood, Ylang-Ylang.

Oils for Normal Skin

Chamomile (For Dry and Sensitve), Fennel (For Oily Skin), Geranium (For all types of skin) Lemon (For Oily Skin), Patchouli (For Dry Skin). Rose (For Dry and Sensitive Skin).

Oils for Oily Skin

Bergamot, Cedarwood, Cypress, Frankincense, Geranium, Juniper, Lavender, Lemon and Sage.

Oils for Sensitive Skin

Chamomile, Lavender, Neroli, Rose and Sandalwood.

In a few cases oils may be required to be blended, particularly when there is combination skin—in some cases skin may be normal from forehead to nose and chin, but dry in other body parts or it could be vice versa also. In this case use oils for the oily skin on greasy areas and use suitable oils for normal skin on the rest of the area of face.

Cleansers and Oils

In this case only correct and suitable essential oils should be choosen that suit best your skin type. Blend suitables oils with unperfumed blend of some cleanser,

tissue, off cream or lotion or liquid soap—
these blended oils will discharge nature's
duty in rebalancing your skin.

Toners

The gentlest way to rejuvenate and tone
up the skin is to use rose oil for dry,
sensitive or normal skin and which hazel
for oily skins—all these can be applied
with cotton wool or sprayed on to the face
for a more refreshing tone. For oral use,
you can use herbal tea in fusions of neetle,
rosehip, chamomile and marigold teas. If
fresh herbs cannot be had, herbal tea bags
may be used instead, dropping 2 drops of
lavender or orange oil and let the same
cool. For dry skins sandalwood or rose oils
would suit better but for oily skins lemon
grass and Juniper are preferred.

Facial Oils

Soft, supple, well-moisturised skin is reflective of healthy glow and also does not age so quickly. Hence use the most suitable facial oil. Most moisturisers sooth and sit on the skin surface while essential oils act from surface to dermis due to their five molecular structure. If the essential oil in requisite proportion to a basic oil, they do not block skin pores on lubrication as they are so light that the skin can immediately absorb them. Add 6 drops of an essential oil to 6 TSP of base oil, keeping in mind an individual's requirements and sensitivity factor but not more than 3 variable oils should be blended with the base oil.

Caution

Sensitivity factor may undergo some change. Hence if an oil is suitable once it should not be taken for granted that the same will suit a person always -such a situation is more common in highly sensitive skins.

Face Masks

Face Masks can be processed from oatmeal and clay. Pulverise fuller's earth that can be mixed into a paste with hot water—let it cool and then add yoghurt to make a smoother consistency. Similarly oatmeal can be reduced a fine powdered form and, then mixed into a paste. Thereafter, add 15 drops of the most suitable essential oil to a cupful of paste and let it cool, thereafter the same paste should be applied to the face. Then leave it to dry a bit and then it should be sponged off. For sensitive/dry skins add 3 TSP of evening primrose to the base oil. Avoid contact with eyes while applying the face mask.

Chapter 11: Aromatherapy Store – Shop For Your Alternative Medical Needs

Arthritis had Mrs. Thompson grounded for years. She had seen several doctors with no permanent solution to the problem. As an alternative medicinal stream, Mrs. Thomson agreed to use aromatherapy. Regular massage with the essential oils of lemon balm, rose, black spruce, tarragon and jasmine was recommended. She testifies to the positive effect aromatherapy had on her condition. Many people like Mrs. Thompson have found relief in aromatherapy treatment. The system of aromatherapy treatment utilizes aromas and scents to heal the human being as a whole. Aromas and scents are derived from several plants and herbs. Research that has been undertaken on plants and herbs from the ancient times until now has helped determine their therapeutic benefits. However, more than a science, aromatherapy is an art and involves a creative approach in making specific blends. Essential oils have an important role to play in aromatherapy treatment.

An essential oil is the essence of plants derived through a process whereby plants are distilled through steam or water. What we get through the process is a concentrated essential oil, of which a few drops are capable of giving the desired effect. One of the first known discoveries of the therapeutic benefits of essential oils was made by French chemist René-Maurice Gattefossé. Gattefossé is also credited with coining the term aromatherapy. When he got a burn on his hand, he accidentally put his hand in a jar full of lavender oil. He was surprised to see that he got immediate relief and the burn left no scars on his hand. Through further research, he established the healing powers of lavender oil. Some of the common ailments where aromatherapy treatment has been accepted as a potent solution are anxiety, stress or insomnia, muscular aches and pains, headaches, eczema, digestive problems, menstrual or menopausal problems, etc. Therefore, aromatherapy treatments heal physically as well as psychologically. A common respiratory disorder is asthma.

This is caused through contact with allergen, after a tiring exercise session or through infection. An asthmatic person experiences shortness of breath, cough and mucous production as a result of inflammation or contraction of the bronchi. The condition can be treated through aromatherapy treatment. The oils of clove bud and lemongrass have been recognized to have anti-inflammatory and anti-infectious properties. These oils along with the oils of lemon, clary sage, and angelica can be very useful for treating asthma. Aromatherapy products are available in several stores, referred to as aromatherapy stores. These stock preparations made from herbs and plants sourced from different parts of the world; mostly, the Indian subcontinent, Middle East and the Africa's. However, the use of aromatherapy treatments must be strictly prescriptive. Toiletries, which use aromas and scents, use a very small amount of essential oils. Therefore, they are not harmful. As said earlier, essential oils are highly concentrated. If a larger dosage of it is taken, then can result in irritation or be poisonous, when used with food or drink.

Did you think essential oils being derived from plants are free from side effects? No, they are not. The common side effects of essential oils are nausea, headaches etc. Get help from an expert practitioner on the appropriate treatment for one's condition. The person who practices aromatherapy treatment is known as aromatherapist. He either will massage the oil on the skin or would suggest the appropriate method of use. Just as one would check the credentials of a doctor practicing in contemporary medicine, it is important to know whether the aromatherapist has been trained in aromatherapy treatment. An aromatherapist proceeds in the same manner as a common doctor. He will first get a detailed medical history of the individual through a series of questions on diet, lifestyle, and health problems. This goes well with the system of aromatherapy healing where the whole rather than one particular ailment is considered for treatment.

Aromatherapy as used today originated in Europe and has been practiced there since the early 1900s. Practitioners of aromatherapy believe that every oil has a vibration or note, which can be used for different therapeutic applications. Aromatherapy can be used to relax and soothe the mind and body, to energize or even to arouse. Aromatherapy derived from the use of essential oils to solicit specific emotions. Essential oils have been used for thousands of years for their health supporting properties. The powerful aromas of essential oils affect your moods and feelings through your sense of smell. By selecting a particular scent, you can encourage a state of relaxation, romance, healing or comfort. Essential oils can be used in Aromatherapy, to scent potpourri, lotions, cosmetics, perfumes, food flavorings and medicinally. Additionally oils can be used in creating sachets, potpourri, reviving potpourri, and for light bulb scenting. Essential oils can also be used via the bath, diffusion, massage, or compress.

Each individual person, fabric, or material may react differently to a particular suggested use. Essential oils can be mixed in a cream essential oil combinations are applied directly to the skin for beauty care or treatment of sores or irritations. By using different essential oils, you can control the nature of those benefits. A unique property of plants is that many contain natural fragrance or perfume-like scents known as essential oils. Essential oils come from plants while fragrance oils are artificially created and often contain synthetic chemicals. Essential oils are taken from a plant's flowers, leaves, stalks, bark, rind, or roots. The yield of essential oil differs with individual plant species-ranging in most cases from about 0.2 to

2.0%. That's why literally tons of plant material is required for just a few hundred pounds of oil. In some cases different organs of a single plant may contain essential oils of different chemical composition. In the end, even the smallest bottle of essential oil can create a lot of powerful solution. It is important to note that the benefits of aromatherapy do depend on the unique nature of each person's response to an aromatic stimulus.

Burning aromatherapy candles scented with pure essential oils is a wonderful way to add fragrance to a room. Not only does an aromatherapy candle smell nice, it can have therapeutic effects on the body and mind. Essential oils are extracted from certain aromatic plants and are used by aromatherapists to promote emotional and physical wellbeing. When a few drops of a particular plant essence are added to a candle, its powerful aroma molecules are diffused into the surrounding air as the wax melts. When inhaled, the fragrance can help soothe and revitalize. Aromatherapy scented candles can be made with oils from various types of plants. Aromatherapy essential oils can be made from different parts of plants, including flowers, berries, leaves and bark. As well as having a unique natural perfume, they have many different healing qualities.

For instance, lavender is well known for its relaxing properties. When added to a jar candle, it can be used to create a soothing and peaceful atmosphere. The rich aroma of sandalwood can help ease feelings of anxiety and stress. As well as being used individually, oils can be used in blends to create uniquely fragranced candles. For example, a seasonal Christmas blend could include mandarin, cinnamon, clove or nutmeg. Or a refreshing mix of oils could include peppermint, lemon, rosemary or bergamot to help stimulate the senses. For maximum aromatherapy benefits, candles should be made from natural based ingredients that don't release toxins as they burn. Aromatherapy soy candles made from soybean wax are a popular option, as these are considered better for the environment than petroleum based candles.

It's worth reading the labels when buying a candle to make sure it contains pure aromatherapy oil and no synthetic fragrances or dyes. Using scented candles in the home is a simple but effective way of influencing the mood of a room, to create a tranquil and harmonious environment. Products such as candles, oil burners or other types of aromatherapy diffusers can make inexpensive gifts and offer a natural alternative to chemical air fresheners. Adding aromatherapy candles to the home is a quick and easy way to enhance the atmosphere in a room and create a peaceful space to unwind in at the end of a busy day.

Chapter 12: Common Methods Of Oil Extraction

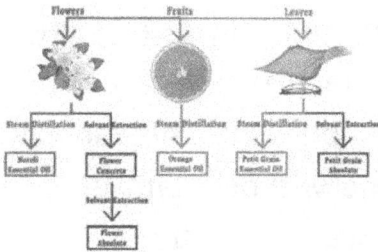

The most intricate and tricky section in the world of aromatherapy is also its most essential one - the process of extraction. When you derive the essence of a natural substance from it, you automatically have several factors that need to be considered. Has the plant material been cultivated the right way? Is it the right time to prepare the plant material for extraction? Can the oils be extracted from the material easily?

And once these questions are answered, there is the actual extraction process. Every plant has a distinct physical structure, and stores its oil deposits in different areas. To get the perfect essential oil, you have to use a means of extraction that can break down the cell walls in the plant to release in the oils from their pockets. This, however, needs to be done without damaging the effects of the plant or altering its chemical structure.

For these purposes, essential oils are mostly extracted on a large-scale basis. The two most common methods used to derive essential oils are steam or water distillation and solvent extraction. Steam distillation and solvent extraction involve placing the plant material either within or above boiling water in a sealed chamber to help extract the essential fumes from the plant. These fumes are collected in a tube and then treated with an ethyl alcohol base to help get the final product.

The problem with these methods, though, is that they need careful monitoring, attention to detail and a specific knowledge of every ingredient involved. And these time-consuming processes may not even give you the amount of oil you require, when undertaken at home.

This doesn't mean that you should try extracting oils at home. There are several methods of extraction that are simple enough to try on easily available plants, like fruit peels, or easily available flowers. Through the following pages, you will learn about three methods - enfleurage, expression and maceration - that help you derive your own oils for aromatherapy from the comfort of your home.

Enfleurage

Enfleurage is an extracted process that was employed in the early days of the perfumery industry. This method was widely practiced in the region of Grasse, France, to extract oils from such flower as jasmine and tuberose.

Oils extracted through these means were highly valued as Enfleurage required vast amounts of work and patience to yield disproportionately low qualities of oil. With the introduction of such modern techniques as solvent extraction, however, Enfleurage became less a less common practice around the world, with Grasse still being one of the last areas known to undertake it.

Enfleurage is one of the gentlest known means of extracting essential oils from plant material. Traditionally, this procedure involved the use of the flower material, along with a readily available form of animal fat or lard. The lard was carefully fit to cover a glass plate - or chassis. The plant material - usually petals from the flower - were then placed and pressed gently onto the lard surface.

The next step required waiting till the oils from the plant material had seeped into the animal fat - this could take days. The plant material was then replaced with a fresh batch and the process was repeated till the fat has absorbed an adequate amount of oil. This oil and wax mixture, called a pomade, was then treated with an ethyl alcohol to separate the fate from the essential oil, resulting in an absolute. This absolute was then diluted and used in therapy and perfumery, while the waxy pomade was used to craft soaps.

Today, this method has been made much simpler and environmentally-conscious by substituting animal fat or lard for a base oil such as olive. Allowing the plant material to float in the base oil for days allows the flower to release oil from its pockets into the container. This infused oil is then treated with ethyl alcohol to separate the absolute from the infusion.

Should you choose to try Enfleurage at home, remember that this process is not labor-intensive, but requires a lot of patience and time. You may find other recipes that tell you infusing the plant material in the base oil yield an essential oil - this is not true. This result is only an infusion - the essence of a plant material is not diluted with other oils and has to be extracted by an agent such as ethyl alcohol. Skipping this alcohol extraction step will give you an oil blend that is not as potent, although it is still therapeutic to an extent.

Oils that can be extracted through this method include flowers such as jasmine, tuberose and lavender.

Maceration

The process of Maceration is that combines the best of Enfleurage with a tweak in the Solvent Extraction method. As with the former, macerating a plant for its essential oil involves soaking the plant material in a carrier oil and then waiting as the oils seep from the plant into the container. The component that distinguishes these two processes is the addition of heat in maceration.

Enfleurage, as we have seen, is used to extract oils from those plant materials that are too volatile or reactive with factors such as heat. When the plant material has a tougher cell membrane that can resist basic reactions, we need to rupture the membrane in order to coax the oil out. A heated base oil is the best means to achieve this without damaging the structure or potency of the essential oil itself.

Like Enfleurage, maceration is a relatively simple extraction procedure to perform at home. Depending on which part of the plant contains the oil, you can use either the whole plant material or the required parts without much preparation. Pay attention to this step as some parts of the plant may contain toxic components not suitable for the human skin.

Another factor to bear in mind during the maceration process is the recommended heat for the base oil. Essential oil can be extracted from different parts of the plant - the stalks, leaves and even roots. Furthermore, the cell membranes of different plants have varied levels of resistance to heat, pressure, light and other variables. Some plants may seep out their oils at relatively low temperatures, while others may need to be soaked in boiling or highly heating oil. Monitor the heating point of your base oils and you should have no problem getting a potent extract.

Oils that can be extracted through the maceration process include plant material such as calendula, carrot, St.John's wort, seaweed, marigold, galangal and horse chestnut.

Expression

The final of the traditional five methods of extracting essential oils is perhaps one off the easiest to perform. Expression, or cold pressing as it commonly known, is the process by which the oil is extracted for the oil-rich rinds of pant material, mostly fruits. Cold pressing is also considered a great way to extract oils from other sources such as nuts and seeds.

Do not be fooled by the appearance of the word "cold" in cold pressing - this is not a heat-free process. While cold pressing will require you to use some measure of heat to help coax the essential oil out from its cell pockets, this heat is relatively low when compared to the other processes of extraction.

When we say cold pressing, we simply mean that the heat applied to the plant material falls between 80 and 120 degrees Fahrenheit - in order to soften up the fleshy oil deposits in the material. The rind, nut or seed is then allowed to set to a cooler temperature before the "pressing" part of the process is undertaken to procure the now loosened oil. The resulting oil may contain some bits from the plant, such as tiny rind pieces, shell fragments or small twigs and seeds. These can easily be filtered away for a clear and pure oil.

The highlight of the cold pressing method is this application of a low heating temperature, as it helps keeps the chemical composition and integrity of the oil intact. The oils extracted through this procedure will often retain their aroma, as well as their color and potency.

Since low levels of heat are required to extract oils through cold pressing, ensure that you pay attention to the temperature on your heating devices, as well as the cooling time required. Along with the quality of plant material used, this attention to heat will affect the quality of your essential oil.

As many manufacturers practice during large-scale expression methods, you can press the same plant material more than once to extract oil until all the oil has seeped out of the cell pockets. Once the first extraction is performed, you simply reheat the plant materials and follow the procedure again till your plant yields no more oil.

This repeated extraction results in oil that may be less potent with each pressing - leading to grades such as "first-pressed", "second-pressed" and so on. If you are purchasing oils extracted through cold processing, try acquiring first-pressed essential oils for the best therapeutic effects.

Oils that can be extracted through the cold pressing methods include citrus plant material such as orange, lime, lemon, grapefruit and bergamot, along with base oils from nuts and seeds like safflower, peanut, flaxseed, pumpkin, sesame, almond and olive.

Chapter 13: Aromatherapy Recipes

Sleep Peacefully

This is a great way to relax and will help you get restful sleep. Millions of us resort to other, unhealthier methods of falling asleep, but this recipe tells you a safe and harmless way to catch some z's at night.

Ingredients:

• 5 drops of Bergamot

• 5 drops of Clary Sage

• 10 drops of Chamomile

Method:

• In a clean glass bottle, add all the essential oils. Shake it well so that the oils are blended evenly.

• Now sprinkle a couple of drops of the oil blend onto tissue paper.

• Place the scented paper underneath your pillow.

Drive That Headache Away!

This recipe can bring almost immediate relief to the headache caused by excessive stress and exhaustion. So before you start popping those pills to make your headache go away, give this recipe a try and see how it can work wonders for you.

Ingredients:

• 5 drops of Frankincense

• 3 drops of Lavender

• 3 drops of Rosewood

• 3 drops of Basil

• 2 drops of Chamomile

• 1 ounce of carrier oil (Jojoba preferably)

Method:

• Blend all the oils into a carrier oil, such as Jojoba.

• Now massage it onto the forehead, temples, and the nape of the neck

• To enhance the effect of this remedy, relax in a calm and dark place.

Relax Those Nerves:

This is a great stress relieving massage mixture, ideal for those suffering from tension in the upper body. It is recommended to ask someone to help you with this massage, but even if you can't get someone to massage your upper body with this oil, it's still possible to do it yourself.

Ingredients:

• 1 drop of Vetiver

• 1 drop of Jasmine

• 3 drops of Marjoram

• 5 drops of Petit grain

• 5 drops of Frankincense

• 60 ml of apricot kernel oil

Method:

• Add all the ingredients in a clean glass bottle.

• Make sure that you shake the bottle well so that the oils blend evenly. You may also roll the bottle between your palms in order to warm up the blend.

• Now massage this blend softly onto the neck and shoulder area using circular motions.

Relieve Pain

With a deep nourishing effect, this blend is an exceptional remedy for those suffering from arthritis and rheumatism. Those affected by the conditions know how debilitating they can be; therefore, using this recipe can help get rid of some of that discomfort. This recipe is also a great way to relax stiff muscles and release muscular tension due to stress.

Ingredients:

• 1 ounce of Balm of Gilead Infused Oil

• 5 drops of Lavender

• 3 drops of Chamomile

- 2 drops of Helichrysum

- 2 drops of Mandarin

- 2 drops of Ginger

- 2 drops of Juniper

Method:

• Mix all the ingredients to make an oil blend.

• Apply the blend to the affected areas to ease pain.

No More Blues

Feeling depressed, withdrawn, or spaced out? This massage recipe will uplift your spirit and melt away your depression right away. Give it a try and see how you can get rid of the blues.

Ingredients:

- 60 ml of Apricot Kernel Oil

- 15 drops of Palmarosa

- 15 drops of Bergamot

- 2 drops of Ylang Ylang

Ingredients:

- Combine all the essential oils with apricot kernel oil in a clean glass bottle.

- Apply the blend all over your body using a circular motion to massage into the skin.

- Pay special attention at the back of the neck, mid-back, and across the shoulders. This will definitely help uplift your mood.

Magical Facial Toner

This recipe has amazing an anti-aging effect and is particularly wonderful for those with sensitive skin. Experience glowing skin in a matter of days with this recipe! This magical toner de-stresses your facial muscles.

Ingredients:

- 3 drops of Lavender

- 3 drops of Sandalwood

- 3 drops of Frankincense

- 1 drop of Chamomile

- 1 tsp of Vegetable Glycerin

- 250 ml of Rose Water

Method:

- Mix all the ingredients in a clean glass bottle and shake gently until well blended.

- Moisten a cotton pad with this blend.

• Now move the pad gently across your face, preferably in a small circular motion. Make sure that you avoid your mouth and eyes.

Wash Away Stress

The best mind is a stress-free mind! Rather than resorting to other conventional and unconventional methods of relieving stress, use this recipe to feel better in a matter of hours.

Ingredients:

• 1 cup of Whole Milk

• 3 drops of Ylang Ylang

• 3 drops of Lavender

• 2 drops of Grapefruit

• 2 drops of Basil

• 2 drops of Geranium

Method:

• Blend the essential oils together with a cup of whole milk.

• Fill the bathtub with warm water and immerse yourself.

• Now add the oil blend and swirl the water in the tub.

• Breathe in the scent of the essential oils and remain in the water for at least 15 minutes.

I Am Focused

Is there a situation that requires intense focus and you're trying hard to gain perspective? Try out this recipe, which promotes focus and mental clarity.

Ingredients:

• 20 drops of Bergamot

- 20 drops of Basil

- 5 drops of Lavender

- 7 drops of Peppermint

- 3 drops of Eucalyptus

Method:

- Add all the ingredients in a bottle and shake well so that they are blended evenly.

- Add 8-12 drops of the oil blend into an electrical diffuser or aroma lamp and inhale the soothing vapors.

Magnificent Marjoram

Marjoram is a fantastic choice to release tension and make you feel good. Try this recipe for a hot bath enriched with essential oils, and remember the golden rule: breathe in relaxation and exhale stress.

Ingredients:

• 3 drops of Marjoram

• 2 drops of Chamomile

• 4 drops of Rosemary

Method:

• Fill your bath tub with comfortably hot water.

• Add all the ingredients in the water and swish them around in the tub.

• Carefully climb in the tub and soak yourself for at least 15 minutes.

• To have an intensified relaxing experience, you may even diffuse any relaxing oil, such as lavender, in your washroom.

Bathe Away The Stress

Lying in this amazing aromatic bath is sure to relax your mind and body after a long, tiring day at work.

Ingredients:

• 15 drops of Almond Oil

• 10 drops of Chamomile

• 7 drops of Lavender

• 2 drops of Clary Sage

Method:

• Blend all the essential oils with almond oil.

• Now add this essential oil blend to a hot bath.

• Step in with your eyes closed and don't forget to take slow deep breaths.

• Stay in the bath for at least 15 minutes. Relax and enjoy!

Soothe That Busy Mind Mist:

This is a fantastic way to help you de-stress and guess what? It takes less than 5 minutes of your hectic schedule.

Ingredients:

• 6 ounces of Distilled Water

• 15 drops of Lavender

• 15 drops of Chamomile

• 4 drops of Vanilla

Method:

• Combine all the ingredients in a clean glass spray bottle.

• Make sure to shake the bottle well so that the oils are mixed properly into the water.

• Spray on as desired.

Easing Stress Rub

Ingredients:

• 9 drops of Bergamot

• 3 drops of Ylang Ylang

• 3 drops of Grape Fruit

Method:

• Combine all the essential oils.

• Drop 4 drops of the blend onto your palm.

• Use your fingertips to apply this blend to the forehead, temples, the back of the neck, and shoulders.

• Massage gently using circular motions.

Stress Busting Foot Soak

Reenergize yourself after a hectic, long day with this relaxing foot bath. It is great for tired and sore feet and works wonders to reduce stress.

Ingredients:

• 3 drops of Lemon

• 3 drops of Peppermint

• 1 tsp of Almond Oil

Method:

• Blend all essential oils with almond oil.

• Fill a tub with warm water.

• Add the mixture into the tub and swirl around to blend evenly before putting your feet in.

• Soak your feet in this aromatic bath for 10 – 15 minutes.

• You may even put 6-8 equal sized marbles in the bottom of the tub with the water (lying down). Moving your feet gently over the marble layer will massage the feet soles and help you relax.

Spa Stress Treatment

Massaging with this oil relieves muscular tension, stimulates circulation, and promotes deep relaxation and stress relief.

Ingredients:

• 1 tbsp of Grape Seed Oil

• 2 drops of Frankincense

• 2 drops of Clary Sage

• 1 drop of Sandalwood

Method:

• Mix the oils with carrier oil, such as grape seed oil, and add to a clean, dark glass bottle.

• Place the blend in your palm and rub over the stress points of the neck, shoulders, and back particularly.

• Make sure you move your fingers in a circular motion. Start the massage gently from the base of the skull, traveling along the neck and toward the shoulder top.

Stress Relieving Salt Bath

Bathing is definitely one of the best stress relieving rituals. This recipe helps relax your tensed nerves and washes away the stress.

Ingredients:

- 1 drop of Ylang Ylang

- 1 drop of Jasmine

- 3 drops of Grapefruit

- 10 ounces of Unscented Bath Salt

Method:

- Pour the drops of these three essential oils in the unscented bath salt. Mix well.

- Add this mixture to the running bath water.

- Stir the bath water before getting in.

Relax, unwind, and enjoy your bath.

Chapter 14: Therapeutic Aromatherapy Recipes

Aromatherapy has a large part to play in therapeutic aromatherapy. Aromatherapy can be used to create many natural remedies.

There are many blends available to treat physical and emotional ailments.

I will provide you with many recipes you can try for yourself and your family.

Preparing Your Essential Oils

We have already discussed different methods of aromatherapy. Essential oils shouldn't be directly applied to the skin in their natural form. Most essential oils will be diluted with carrier oil, or water in order to achieve a concentration of between 3% and 5.

If you have 1 teaspoon of carrier oil, add 3 to 5 drops of essential oil. You will need to shake the carrier oil every time you apply it.

Safety data regarding essential oils and essential oil mixtures should be reviewed regularly, especially if you take prescriptions or other medication.

5 Methods of Application

Compress

Use carrier oil or water to dilute the essential oil. Apply the oil to the area. Before applying the dressing, you can also apply a dressing. You can apply the compress hot or cold.

Bath

Your essential oils can be added directly to your bath water, depending on the recipe. The oils should be added just before you get into the tub. This allows essential oils to be absorbed into your skin. You will also have the added benefit of inhaling them.

Gargle

You can add a few drops to your essential oil to the water. Mix the essential oil with water and then gargle as normal. Do not swallow the mixture. Start with a small amount and increase the quantity as you go. This will help you find the right strength, so it's not too strong.

Diffuser Blends

To get the right strength for a diffuser, multiply your blend by four times. Follow the manufacturer's directions.

Massage

A 1% solution will suffice to massage larger areas of the body. One teaspoon of oil would yield one drop of essential oil.

These are the best ways to make the following therapeutic blends.

20 20.

These blends can be helpful when you're angry.

Blend #1

6 drops bergamot

3 drops of ylang-ylang

3 drops jasmine

Blend #2

3 drops rose

2 drops orange

2 drops of vetiver

Blend #3

4 drops patchouli

3 drops orange

Blend #4

5 drops of orange

3 drops bergamot

2 drops Roman Chamomile

21.Recipes for Calming Anxiety

If you have anxiety, these blends can help.

Blend #1

5 drops lavender

3 drops clary Sage

Blend #2

4 drops bergamot

3 drops frankincense

2 drops clary Sage

Blend #3

4 drops lavender

2 drops mandarin

2 drops rose

2 drops of vetiver

Blend #4

6 drops bergamot

2 drops sandalwood

22.Recipes for Increasing Confidence

These blends can help increase your confidence.

Blend #1

3 drops of cypress

2 drops grapefruit

Blend #2

4 drops rosemary

2 drops orange

Blend #3

8 drops bergamot

6 drops jasmine

Blend #4

5 drops bergamot

2 drops bay laurel

23.Recipes for Relaxation and Calm

These blends can help you relax and calm down.

Blend #1

4 drops frankincense

2 drops Roman Chamomile

3 drops lavender

Blend #2

12 drops Roman Chamomile

3 drops lavender

24.Recipes that Ease Depression

These blends can be used to help with depression.

Blend #1

6 drops sandalwood

2 drops orange

2 drops rose

Blend #2

5 drops bergamot

2 drops clary Sage

Blend #3

4 drops frankincense

2 drops lemon

2 drops jasmine

1 drop neroli

Blend #4

4 drops of ylang-ylang

2 drops lavender

1 drops grapefruit

25.Recipes for Increasing Energy

These blends can help you increase your energy.

Blend #1

5 drops rosemary

3 drops bergamot

Blend #2

3 drops frankincense

2 drops lemon

1 drop peppermint

Blend #3

5 drops ginger

1 drop grapefruit

Blend #4

3 drops of cypress

2 drops grapefruit

2 drops basil

Menstrual Cramps: A Recipe

There are many essential oils that can be used to ease cramps and other symptoms related to menstrual problems. Do not be afraid to try new things. You can add a few drops of the oil to a warm bath, along with some Epsom salt. Or you can use a carrier oil to rub your abdomen.

Essential oils for menstrual cramps

Lavender

Chamomile

Frankincense

Peppermint

Jasmine

Rosemary

Clary Sage

Basil

Cypress

Juniper

Marjoram

Nutmeg

How to reduce the symptoms of cold and flu

What you need:

Large bowl

Towel

Ingredients:

10 drops eucalyptus essential oil

6 drops scotch pine essential oil

6 drops lemon essential oil

Boiling water

Instructions

Boil the water, then pour it into a large bowl.

All essential oils should be added to the steaming water.

Place a towel over your head and support the bowl. For 5-6 minutes, inhale deeply.

Vaginal Dryness Recipe

What you need:

Mixing bowl

Glass jar that seals

Ingredients:

2 ounces melted chocolate butter

4 ounces parts jojoba oil

5 drops sandalwood essential oil

2 drops geranium or neroli essential oil

Instructions

The cocoa butter should be melted. Next, add the jojoba oils.

Add essential oils.

Mix well by heating.

Let the mixture cool in a glass container. The mixture will begin to solidify.

Smooth the cream on the tissue twice daily using your fingers. For a more comfortable intercourse, you can also use the cream just before it.

How to Fight Germs

This is an excellent antiseptic and germ fighting spray you can use to disinfect hands, clean cuts, and spray a room. It is safer and more effective than most commercial products.

What you need:

Spray bottle

Ingredients:

30 drops of tea tree essential oil

15 drops eucalyptus essential oil

10 drops lemon essential oil

8 ounces of distilled water

Instructions

Combine all ingredients in a spray bottle.

Before using, shake the container.

How to Stop Snoring

Thyme has been proven to be beneficial for snorers. Others have reported better results with lavender, peppermint and eucalyptus. Apply the oil to your feet.

It can be used to treat your throat and nasal region. You can experiment to find the best way to get the best results. If you can stop snoring, it's well worth the effort.

How to make your own "Vapor-Rub".

What you need:

Glass jar with seal

Saucepan

Spoon

Ingredients:

8 Tbsp. 8 Tbsp.

4 Tbsp. Olive oil

20 Tbsp. Coconut oil

Essential oil of rosemary: 40 drops

20 drops of tea tree essential oil

Instructions

Take out the beeswax.

Melt the coconut oil, beeswax, and olive oil in a saucepan.

Mix the essential oils well.

Take off heat and pour into glass jars

Allow to cool, then seal.

Cough syrup recipe

Warm cough syrup can be taken by the teaspoon or mixed with hot water or tea.

The coconut oil will harden when the cough syrup cools.

It can be kept in the fridge and heated up when needed. It will last for 4-6 weeks.

What you need:

Saucepan

Glass container with lid for storage

Ingredients:

12 drops of essential oil lemon

1 cup of local raw honey

8 Tbsp. Coconut oil

Instructions

Combine all ingredients in a saucepan.

Turn heat to low until all ingredients are melted. Stir constantly.

Place in a glass container and seal.

Recipe for Ear Infection

Most doctors still use antibiotics to treat ear infections. We know that antibiotics are out of control, and that there are potential risks.

Here are some options for you and your child if you have an ear infection.

The cotton ball method: Take a few drops of tea tree or lavender essential oils and place them on a cotton band.

Place the cotton ball in your ear and gently take it. Change the cotton ball every 3-4 days.

Keep going with the treatment until you are satisfied. Do not put essential oils directly in the ear.

Calendula oil - Calendula oil will draw out heat. Place one drop of oil on the outside of your ear and massage it into your ear. Do not put essential oils directly in the ear.

Lemon essential oil - Lemon can soothe ear infections. This is often enough to drain the fluid.

Mix 2-3 drops of lemon essential oils with equal amounts of coconut oil.

The coconut oil should be melted. Next, mix the essential oil with it and rub the area around your ear.

Cover your lymph nodes on the sides of your neck. Essential oils should never be injected directly into the ears.

Natural Home Care Recipes

Many people don't know that aromatherapy and essential oils can be used to create a natural, chemical-free home environment. This can create a more harmonious environment, and can also help with your emotions. Many people don't consider the negative effects of chemicals we are constantly exposed to and how they can affect our minds and bodies.

There are many products that can be used to keep your home clean and fresh. You can use laundry detergent, bleach, window cleaner, general cleaning products, and many more. Here are some great recipes that will help you get started.

When you have a safe home environment, you will be able to make safer aromatherapy home care products. There are many recipes out there, so this is a good place to start.

Natural laundry detergent recipe

What you need:

Measure spoon

Airtight glass container

Food processor

Cheese grater

Ingredients:

5 bars (4.5 oz. or 5 oz. Castile soap

3 cups borax

5 cups of washing soap

45 drops either of the lavender or lemon essential oils

Instructions

All soap bars should be grated

Blend all ingredients together.

Blend the ingredients until well combined.

Keep the laundry detergent in an airtight container.

For each load, you will need to use 2-3 tablespoons of detergent

Homemade Bleach Recipe

What you need:

A gallon jug

Ingredients:

Distilled water for filling a gallon jug

2 cups lemon juice

6 cups 3% hydrogen peroxide

25-30 drops lemon essential oil

Instructions

Combine all ingredients in a gallon jug.

Gently mix.

To whiten and brighten clothes, add 1 cup to the washing machine.

Chapter 15: What's the Deal?

Synopsis

There are many virtues to the popular belief that stress, anxiety, and inadequate daily nutrition are responsible for most diseases and illnesses.

Unfortunately, some diseases and illnesses must reach a critical stage before they become visible or are detected. It is possible to prevent this from happening, but it can be difficult.

This is where aromatherapy can be helpful. Aromatherapy is best known for its relaxing properties. It uses essential oils to soothe the mind and body. Aromatherapy can also be used to treat other conditions.

Some Healing

Here are just a few examples that illustrate the benefits and capabilities of aromatherapy.

Apply tea tree oil or lavender oil directly to the affected area. A body lotion with these properties can be used for milder cases.

Anemia can be caused by a combination of tincture of the yellow dock root and an extract of dandelion leaves, or even eating dandelion greens in a salad.

Anxiety - California poppy, passion flower and lemon balm.

Asthma - Ginkgo biloba and mullein oil. A Chinese herb called Shuan huanglian is also available.

Bee sting - cantharis, lavendar, and vegetable oil mixed

Alfalfa has chlorophyll which can cause body odor.

Inhale cold - warm eucalyptus oil with boiling water. Mixture of tea tree oil and water can be added to the gargle.

Cholesterol, chicory root and ginger

Constipation - aloe vera juice, ginger tea

Hair loss - saw palmetto, arnica, jojoba oil

Headaches - chamomile relaxes, ginkgo biloba improves blood circulation

Dandruff: Flaxseed oil (primrose oil, salmon oil) Chaparral or thyme shampoo for hair.

Diabetes - Huckleberry tea, made from most beans

Diarrhea: blackberry tea, wild oregano

Eczema: Chickweed added to bath. Stinging nettle, hazel Ointment

Indigestion - gentian root for better digestion, ginger, peppermint

Nausea, vomiting - Catnip leaves, Chamomile flowers

Chapter 16: Lavender Linen Spray

Aromatic, Safe For All Ages, Must Have

Not many people iron clothes these days. Next time you want to enjoy the luxury of freshly ironed clothes or table linens, though, treat yourself to a quick aromatherapy session, well imparting a lovely sent.

Makes: 1 cup

Ingredients

• 30 drops lavender essential oil

• 1 cup Water, distilled

Instructions

• In a bottle fitted with a spray top, combine the lavender essential oil and distilled water. Cap the bottle and shake well before use. Shake again if you notice the lavender floating to the top during use.

• Set your iron's temperature to the appropriate level for the fabric you are ironing.

• Lightly spritz your items and iron them.

• Keep the linen spray in a cool, dark place between uses.

Energizing essential oil blend

In today's lifestyle and environment conditions, we barely have enough time for everything that we want to do. There's work that you need to finish in the office and there are chores you have to do to maintain your home. There's a wide range of stimulants that you can use to help keep you going, but barely any of them have positive health effects in the long run. Stuff like caffeine and cigarettes can give you the quick energy boost you want, but for a price. If you don't want to get sick after years of taking stimulants, or if you're tired of getting sick because of them, we've got the solution for you. We have a recipe for an essential oil blend that can boost your energy, focus your mind, and uplift your spirits.

Ingredients:

- 3 drops of grapefruit essential oil

- 3 drops of lemon essential oil

- 2 drops of spearmint essential oil

Spearmint essential oil in particular can stimulate your senses and improve your concentration. Lemon essential oil is responsible for rejuvenation and is popular for its calming effects. However, the best thing about lemon essential oil is its ability to stimulate your brain to break down body fat. Aside from helping you get your dream bod, it can also reduce tension and relieve exhaustion and mental fatigue. Grapefruit essential oil boosts your energy levels, but it's also used to improve your metabolism and reduce bad cholesterol. It can reduce fatigue by stimulating your nervous system to make you feel more alert while it detoxifies your body. You can use this blend with a diffuser, or adapt it for things like massage oil blends or DIY scented candles.

Spiritual blend

Plants and aromatics have been used in spiritual practices since time immemorial. Essential oils can also play a role in helping you enhance or embrace your spirituality. All essential oils are aromatic, but some are more suited for spiritual uses than others. If you're interested in incorporating essential oils into your spiritual practices, you can explore which scents work for you the best. However, we can also give you a head start by giving you a recipe for a spiritual aromatherapy essential oils blend. Here's a blend that you can start with:

- 2 drops of cedarwood essential oil

- 2 drops of patchouli essential oil

- 2 drops of ylang ylang essential oil

- 1 drop of rosemary essential oil

You can play around with the amounts of each essential oil and adjust them until you get the exact balance of scents that you prefer. Cedarwood essential oil is one of the oldest essential oils in the world. It is perhaps one of the best essential oils you can use for spiritual practices because of its grounding and purifying properties. It can clear your mind and release negativity. Patchouli essential oil can help cleanse your space of negative energies. It is regenerative, restorative, and protective, making it an important addition to this aromatherapy blend. Just like cedarwood, the earthy patchouli is perfect for grounding.

Ylang ylang essential oil is known to be healing and relaxing, making it great for meditative purposes. Furthermore, it can bring balance to your mind, body, and spirit. Its lush floral scent is also a great bonus.

Rosemary essential oil is protective and purifying, making it a great oil to use if you want to cleanse your space. It can help release psychic and spiritual blocks, as well as rejuvenate and sharpen your mind. In addition, it's also believed to provide good fortune.

Car aromatherapy blend

Many of us spend a lot of time in cars, driving to and from work, appointments, and errands. Fortunately, it's actually possible to have an aromatherapy session even when you're in your car and on your way to the office, the doctor's office, or a grocery store. If you're always on the go and your schedule is full, you can squeeze in a car aromatherapy session while you're stuck in traffic or while you're on a long road trip. These aromatherapy recipes can help you stay calm yet alert, however long your drive may be.

You can start with this car aromatherapy blend. Here are the essential oils you'll need:

- 5 drops of eucalyptus essential oil

- 2 drops of lemon essential oil

- 1 drop of mandarin essential oil

- 2 drops of spearmint essential oil

This blend is great for car diffusers, but you can also check out more car aromatherapy recipes. Eucalyptus essential oil can help you stay alert and refreshed, which can be really useful if you're driving late at night or early in the morning. It helps relieve mental sluggishness, which prevents you from making errors in driving. As a bonus, eucalyptus can also help make your car smell fresh and new. Lemon essential oil can help clear your mind and sharpen your focus. This can help you concentrate better on your driving, which can help you ignore distractions. Furthermore, lemon essential oil can help keep you calm, making it a great scent for new or nervous drivers. Mandarin essential oil can also help keep you calm without making you feel tired or sleepy. It can help ease anxiety or nerves while keeping your senses sharp and alert. Additionally, its fresh scent can also be helpful in long drives or older cars.Spearmint essential oil has a cool and refreshing aroma that isn't as strong as its cousin's, peppermint. It can also help reduce feelings of nausea, which can be helpful to those that suffer from motion sickness. This scent can therefore make car rides easier and more comfortable.

Anti-anxiety blend

If you're battling anxiety, we give you a natural way to fight back. You can use this recipe any time of the day, unlike anti-anxiety medicines that can have adverse long-term effects on your brain. However, it's important to note that essential oils are not cures for anxiety. Instead, they can give you a way to reduce the effects of your anxiety and allow you to deal with the symptoms better. In fact, there is a study about the effects of using essential oils to improve depression and anxiety management among research subjects. The essential oils were diluted with sweet almond oil then topically applied as a hand massaging oil. The subjects were then interviewed, and they reported experiencing less pain with the aromatherapy massage:

Ingredients

• 4 drops of tangerine essential oil

• 2 drops of ylang ylang essential oil

• 2 drops of bergamot essential oil

Tangerine essential oil has calming and sedative properties. If you're prone to anxiety and nervousness, this oil can help you calm down and keep a clear head. It can also help you release tension, making it easier for you to relax.

Ylang ylang essential oil is one of the best-known calming essential oils. It has a floral aroma that can help induce calmness and optimism. Furthermore, it's versatile and can be used in perfumes, massage oils, and more.

Bergamot essential oil can lower heart pressure and reduce the production of the hormone called corticosterone that induces stress responses. Additionally, it can help reduce heart rate, which can in turn help you feel more calm physically and mentally.

Brain boost blend

Have you been feeling a bit out of focus lately? We all have our ups and downs, especially in the creativity department. However, if your work involves a lot of thinking, then you'll need all the focus that you can get. There are a lot of things you can do to keep you away from distractions. You can stay off your phone, keep your desk clear, or work in a quiet environment, to name a few. However, there are times when even these measures may not be enough. You can thus try this essential oil blend that can help you boost your memory, improve your focus, and enhance your concentration.

Ingredients:

• 8 drops of rosemary essential oil

• 4 drops of sage essential oil

• 3 drops of basil essential oil

• 3 drops of lemon essential oil

Rosemary essential oil improves memory and alertness. It also has properties that improve your brain's ability to retain information. A whiff of this amazing oil can enhance your cognitive performance and prevent neurodegeneration. Sage essential oil, like rosemary, can also help improve memory and recall. It can be a particularly helpful oil if you're preparing for a test, a presentation, or anything else that requires the memorization of details. Basil is another stimulating essential oil that helps your mental strength and gives you clarity. It can reduce anxiety, nervousness, and fatigue. In fact, it's used to improve focus and fight chronic stress, which can help you keep calm while staying focused. Lemon essential oil has been found to be able to not just help improve memory, but improve efficiency as well. This is especially helpful for time-sensitive tasks, or if you'd just like to get more things done in a shorter period of time.

Conclusion

Essential oils are generally considered safe to inhale or apply to the skin if they've been combined with a base oil. They should not be eaten. However, evidence supporting many of their associated health claims is lacking, and their effectiveness is often exaggerated. For minor health problems, using essential oils as a complementary therapy is likely harmless.

However, if you have a serious health condition or are taking medication, you should discuss their use with your healthcare practitioner. As you explore the uses of essential oils, pay attention to how the different oils and methods of use affect you. Always talk to your doctor before starting any aromatherapy treatment. Remember that aromatherapy is meant to be a complementary therapy.

It's not meant to replace any doctor-approved treatment plan . Essential oils are concentrated plant extracts that retain the natural smell and flavor, or "essence," of their source.

Essential oils can be inhaled or diluted and applied to the skin. They may stimulate your sense of smell or have medicinal effects when absorbed. There are over 90 commonly used essential oils, each associated with certain health claims. Popular oils include peppermint, lavender, and sandalwood.

Essential oils may have some interesting health applications. However, more research is needed in humans. Essential oils are generally considered safe. However, they may cause serious side effects for some people, especially if applied directly to the skin or ingested.

Essential oils are made by distilling the roots, stems, leaves, flowers, and bark of plants with steam or water. These highly concentrated oils are then inhaled, ingested, or can be applied to the skin through a lotion, cream, or oil.